FRAMEWORK PROCESS PATTERNS

Lessons Learned Developing Application Frameworks

D1736702

FRAMEWORK PROCESS PATTERNS
Lessons Learned Developing Application Frameworks

James Carey

Brent Carlson

✦▾Addison-Wesley

Boston • San Francisco • New York • Toronto • Montreal
London • Munich • Paris • Madrid
Capetown • Sydney • Tokyo • Singapore • Mexico City

The publisher offers discounts on this book when ordered in quantity for special sales. For more information, please contact:

Pearson Education Corporate Sales Division
201 W. 103rd Street
Indianapolis, IN 46290
(800) 428-5331
corpsales@pearsoned.com

Visit Addison-Wesley on the Web: www.aw.com/cseng/

Library of Congress Control Number: 2002101207

ISBN 0-201-73132-0

Text printed on recycled paper

1 2 3 4 5 6 7 8 9 10—CRS—0605040302

First printing, April 2002

Contents

Preface

What does it take to create object-oriented application frameworks? How do you create something that provides the core of an application and does it in a way that can be used to build many applications? Object-oriented programming skills are a great start, but they just aren't enough to create a successful framework. So what else do you need?

Many of you underwent a change when you went from procedural programming to object-oriented programming. Until you made that change, you could write in Java (or C++), but you weren't actively doing object-oriented programming (except by accident). You gained experience through reading books and being mentored (and making mistakes), which transformed you. You internalized a set of patterns for object-oriented programming—patterns that helped you use proper inheritance, patterns that made your designs truly object-oriented, and patterns that helped you form effective development teams. Becoming a framework developer involves a similar transition. It isn't as large a transition, but it is still a transition.

What makes frameworks unique? Frameworks are a balancing act between providing reusable content (for example, prebuilt business objects and processes for business applications) and flexibility (allowing that content to be customized to do exactly what the framework user wants). This is a very delicate balancing act. When too much flexibility is provided, the framework splinters into small confederations of business objects with low-level processes—very much like a class library. On the other hand, if too much content is provided, we risk complicating customization to the point where no one will be able to use it—very much like trying to use an existing application to write another. Learning how to effectively find this balance point is what the transition to becoming a framework developer is about.

To help you make this transition, this book contains the essence of what we learned as we became framework developers. We've distilled key aspects of our experiences into patterns that you can immediately apply to your work—patterns that we believe are valuable not only to anyone working with frameworks (developing, using, or evaluating them) but also to other software developers. Framework development tested and intensified what we learned during our transition to object-oriented developers; thus we feel that object-oriented developers will benefit. Also, with the development of more and more customizable applications, components, and Web services, the patterns about teams of technical (nondomain) and nontechnical (domain) experts working together to develop software are becoming increasingly applicable.

This book isn't about object-oriented development or how to program in a particular object-oriented language. It doesn't describe arcane algorithms, radically new development processes, or arguments for a new way to model object-oriented designs. Instead, we've captured (as patterns) situations that we've encountered (and that typically occur) during normal object-oriented framework development. We cover the range of development activities from initial requirements gathering to documenting the framework. We also spend some time on the human side of development—how to deal with the interactions among all the different types of people who need to work together to make a software development project successful. Finally, we briefly look at using a framework to develop an application.

You will get the most value from this book if you have experience in object-oriented development. If you are new to object-oriented programming, you will still find this book valuable—it will expose you to a number of issues you will encounter in the future. This book will be useful to framework developers and framework users. Framework users will benefit not only from learning patterns specific to using the framework but also by knowing what should have gone into the development of the framework. Managers of object-oriented development projects will find this book useful because it points out some of the potential pitfalls and significant issues development teams have to deal with throughout the software development process.

What are these patterns? The Tor's Second Cousin pattern (see Section 4.2), for example, is named after Tor, one of the domain experts working on the IBM SanFrancisco frameworks. Tor had the ability to identify cases where the framework needed flexibility that no one else had considered. We attributed these revelations to his fictitious (and crazy) second cousin. In many cases, these scenarios represented requirements that were, simply put, too flexible. In other words, only a minuscule percentage of the applications built using the framework would ever need to use the framework in the way Tor described. As development leaders in the project, we had to make hard decisions whenever these cases came up: should we include support for such flexible requirements in the framework or not? The Tor's Second Cousin pattern captures making this tradeoff between flexibility and complexity. Flexibility that is needed by some small portion of the framework's target audience but that requires additional complexity in the framework should be avoided. This rule provided a way to look at these situations without anyone taking offense. Asking if a requirement came from Tor's second cousin didn't imply that the requirement was invalid or that the person who suggested the requirement was stupid or out of line; it merely caused us to make sure that we considered the complexity/flexibility tradeoff. By giving this rule a humorous name, we were also able to defuse tensions that might have otherwise arisen as people debated the requirement. We have found that humor, when properly applied, is extremely effective in building a team and reducing tension, especially in the stressful environment that results from developing software under great time pressures. For these reasons most of the patterns presented in this book have humorous names in addition to their more descriptive names. For example, the Tor's Second Cousin pattern is also known as How Extreme Is Too Extreme?

Why process patterns? Scott Ambler defines a process pattern as a proven, successful approach to developing software [Ambler 99]. In this book we provide proven, successful approaches to developing frameworks. Capturing them as patterns allows us to document them in a consistent manner so that you can easily examine the pattern and its applicability and determine whether it can be applied to your particular situation or possibly used as a starting point for defining your own solution. Each pattern has the following sections:

> **Name**—The name of the pattern—usually humorous
>
> **Also Known As**—Other names by which the pattern is known
>
> **Intent**—What the pattern is about, briefly
>
> **Context**—The motivation for the pattern
>
> **Examples**—Examples, normally based on the case study
>
> **Problem**—A concise statement of the problem the pattern addresses
>
> **Approaches**—Various solutions, some of which may be raised and then knocked down, again normally based on the case study

Solution—A concise statement of how the pattern recommends solving the problem

When to Use/Not to Use—Tradeoffs of the pattern, normally based on the case study

Applicability—A concise statement of the tradeoffs

Known Uses—Places the pattern was applied—including IBM SanFrancisco framework examples

Related Patterns—Other patterns related to the current one and how they are related

Why Listen to Us?

Like many of you, we began as procedural programmers. We were taught object-oriented techniques in the classroom and then tempered our skills in the furnace of experience. We both worked on building portions of an object-oriented operating system in C++. These pieces were part of the project that moved the AS/400 from a CISC to a RISC processor base in the early 1990s. This project involved changing or replacing over a million lines of code. Most of the organization was new to object-oriented development, so we didn't concentrate just on our own designs and code. Instead, the team members were very open and helped one another by discussing and reviewing each other's designs and code. By the time we completed the CISC to RISC conversion, we were both very experienced object-oriented developers. This is the starting point for the experiences captured in this book.

Where did we go from there? We were both brought onto the IBM SanFrancisco project to develop distributed object-oriented business application frameworks in Java. The goal was to produce something that would provide application developers the core of their applications—in other words, the part everyone does: the ante to play the game. The framework would allow application developers to spend more time making an application unique, adding those things that differentiate it from its competitors, rather than simply keeping up by providing what everyone provides. The framework would allow application developers to customize framework elements for their unique requirements.

The SanFrancisco frameworks were delivered as a number of layers. At the bottom were the more traditional, technically oriented frameworks that supported things such as persistence and distributed objects (much of which is now provided by Java's Enterprise JavaBeans[1]). Built on these technical frameworks were the business application frameworks. These frameworks, instead of capturing reusable technical solutions, captured reusable business content—business objects and business processes. The frameworks were further divided into those applicable across most, if not all, domains and those targeted as specific domains, such as warehouse management or accounting. Although we were involved with development of all the layers, our main focus was the business application frameworks that captured business content.

The SanFrancisco development team chose to use object-oriented techniques for all the standard reasons: effective isolation and decomposition of complexity, improved maintainability, and partitioning of development effort into self-contained chunks, among others [Booch 94]. One especially appealing reason was that object-oriented techniques allow responsibilities to be encapsulated into objects. Thus we could make the scope of change in any one part of the framework limited and understandable, something key to a framework that expects changes for customization. We chose Java because it would allow the application the most flexibility in terms of platforms.

When we finished the project, the IBM SanFrancisco frameworks had over 1,000 business-oriented classes and nearly 1,000,000 lines of Java code, making the IBM SanFrancisco frameworks the largest commercial object-oriented business application framework ever completed and sold.

What do lots of classes and code have to do with listening to us? Directly, not much. What they show is that we have had to use framework techniques to solve a lot of problems. We didn't simply write one small framework and declare a pattern because we saw something once—or because we thought it might be a pattern. We identified these patterns because we saw them over and over again. They were identified, refined, and used by the entire team, a team of both technical and domain experts. Finally, numerous software developers have validated these patterns by building flexible applications, both for broad resale and for very specific business needs, on top of the IBM SanFrancisco frameworks.

---

1. For more information, see http://java.sun.com/products/ejb.

How to Read This Book

All readers should read Chapters 1 and 2 (the Introduction and Case Study chapters). The Introduction provides the underlying context of the patterns by describing what a framework is, how it is developed, and how it is used. It shows how the patterns fit together and gives you a starting point from which you can go to those patterns that interest you. The Case Study chapter provides a common domain and vocabulary from which we can present the problems that lead to the patterns and the approaches to solving them.

Once you've read the Introduction and Case Study chapters, you can read the remaining chapters in any order. Managers or developers trying to get an overview of the patterns should consider reading the Intent, Problem, Solution, and Applicability sections for all the patterns. The remaining sections can then be read when going back and reading the chapter in detail, possibly focusing first on those patterns that seem to be the most applicable.

Related patterns have been collected together into chapters that identify their primary application.

- Chapter 3 discusses the patterns that apply across the entire framework development process.
- Chapter 4 discusses the patterns related to identifying and capturing requirements.
- Chapter 5 continues with the development process by looking at patterns from the analysis phase.
- Chapter 6 covers the design-phase patterns.
- Chapter 7 discusses the patterns associated with documentation. Extensive documentation is crucial when developing frameworks.
- Chapter 8 discusses the social aspects of developing frameworks (and general object-oriented software), including patterns unique to domain and technical expertise residing in separate people.
- Chapter 9 discusses patterns related to using the framework.

Two appendixes are included. Appendix A describes the complementary relationship between components and frameworks. Appendix B describes the process used to develop the business application frameworks as part of the IBM SanFrancisco project.

Acknowledgments

We did not come up with these rules on our own. They are the result of the team effort that developed the IBM SanFrancisco frameworks. Each member of the team contributed in some way to the experiences from which these rules sprung. We want to thank each and every one of the team members—you were one of the best teams with which we've ever worked.

Brent thanks his wife, Lisa, for her willingness to tolerate his book-writing hobby, and he promises not to sign any more book contracts anytime soon!

Jim thanks his family for supporting him through the long hours of work on this book.

We both want to thank our reviewers: Michele Chilanti, Will Traz, Simon Reason, Palle Nowack, Marcus Fontoura, and Roger Snowden for helping us focus and refine the book into what it is today. We also thank all the people at Addison-Wesley who made this book possible, especially Paul Becker and Marcy Barnes. Finally, a special thanks to Chrysta Meadowbrooke for turning our technical gibberish into proper English.

James Carey

Brent Carlson

Chapter

1

Introduction

For someone familiar with object-oriented development, developing an object-oriented framework will be both familiar and new. It will be familiar because framework development stresses the lessons of good object-oriented development and new because it brings new challenges and surprises. One of the biggest challenges is accepting that an object-oriented framework involves delivering more than the executable code and limited documentation you've developed before.

1.1 What Is a Framework?

In *Design Patterns,* Gamma et al. provide the following definition of a framework: "A framework is a set of cooperating classes that make up a reusable design for a specific class of software" [Gamma 94, p. 26]. Extending this definition just a bit, we say that a framework is a set of components working together so they address a number of problems in one or more domains. These definitions are essentially the same. These definitions share key aspects.

- A framework involves a number of abstractions—classes or components.
- These abstractions cooperate or work together to do something. A framework takes a team of individual abstractions and defines how they work together. This definition is the reusable core (design and implementation) of the solution.

- The abstractions and how they do what they do are reusable. A framework isn't a class library. A class library's purpose is to provide a set of classes and functions that are common almost to the point of being ubiquitous. A framework provides reuse at the next level up for processes and functions that are "almost" common. In fact, a framework can be built on top of a class library, providing this next level on top of it. Although a framework should rely heavily on design patterns, a framework isn't just a group of patterns. It is the combination of designs and implementations, targeted to meet a set of needs in a general way (see our next point), and built on a core architecture that can be extended (customized) to fit the needs of different uses. The places where this extension is supported are called *extension points* (also called *hotspots*).

- The framework addresses a specific area. A framework must have a target area it addresses (a domain). What if it doesn't? What if you created the ultimate framework that could be used to build anything? Actually, it's too late—not only have you been beaten to the punch but there are lots to choose from, all called *programming languages*. A programming language provides a set of abstractions (primitives) that cooperate (operations) and are all reusable to write any program you want. OK, it was a trick question, but it makes an important point. A framework can't be everything to everybody. It must address a specific set of objectives. This book helps you explore how to pick the objectives and understand what that means to the framework development process. We can't pick the objectives for you, but we can give you some patterns to help you decide what objectives are right for you and help you to focus on those objectives.

Before considering something to be a framework, it should meet each of these criteria in some way. It isn't good enough to simply say the framework addresses the domain of constructing celestial bodies (planets and so on), to pick an absurd example. We have to be able to do it! We have to provide the framework in such a way that it consists of abstractions that work together and can be reused (extended) to address the domain (celestial bodies in this case). Can we write a framework that addresses the complete planet domain? Probably not, and even if we could, we probably don't want to pay to do it. On the other hand, we should know which celestial bodies we want to create and can thus scope down the domain to a subset of all possible bodies. For example, we could choose to create only simple nongaseous planets. It's a tradeoff, though: we are deciding that when we have to create a gaseous planet or a planet with rings or moons, we won't get the benefit of the framework. However, the good side is that this focus reduces the complexity of the framework. Now the framework can be more focused and can omit the support for customization (extension) needed to create planets that have rings or moons. This example, although absurd, points out the importance of excluding outlying conditions, a topic explored in more detail in the Tor's Second Cousin pattern (see Section 4.2).

1.2 Framework Artifacts

As mentioned before, one of the greatest challenges is realizing that most of the framework artifacts must be delivered to the customer. As when developing other software, it is sufficient to document only those places where the customer is likely to work with the software. The difference is that for other software this usually occurs at a few well-defined interfaces. For a framework, the customer works with almost all aspects of the software. The customer needs to understand the requirements, use cases, analysis model, design model, design decisions, programming model, patterns used, and so on. You may even provide the source code to the customer. Suddenly all of these things that were hidden (or not formally produced) in the past are part of your product. The key is realizing that you are a partner with the framework users. You are partnering together to help them develop and deliver their application, and you need to do whatever you can to make them successful.

In addition to the development-level artifacts, a number of other documents need to be considered: documents that help different audiences understand and use the framework. One that we have found extremely important is a document that helps a nontechnical domain expert understand the capabilities of the framework. For example, domain-level user guides should use the terminology that domain experts in the field use, not the technical terms used by developers.

This documentation might also take the form of usage samples, showing how to complete the framework (by using the extension points) to solve specific application requirements. These examples need to work properly so they can be used as a starting point to help framework users understand the framework and then adjust it to their particular needs.

Tooling should also be considered. These tools can range from development tools that help generate code to wizards that help create the framework extensions to support a particular framework user's needs.

Determining the exact artifacts to provide with your framework involves a number of factors (see the Exposing It All pattern, Section 3.6), not the least of which is the time allotted to developing the framework. The important thing to realize is that there will be more artifacts than with other software.

1.3 Developing Frameworks

Developing a framework involves more than just the product (that is, what you are going to ship as part of the framework, its architecture, and how it is factored). It also encompasses the process used to develop the framework (including the evolutionary iterations), the development team and organization that developed it, and the customer using it (including the business models and processes supported by the framework). All of these factors need to be taken into account during framework development and should be captured as part of your development process. Ignoring any of these factors is likely to result in disaster.

Development Process

Developing frameworks is both similar to and different from developing applications. In either case, you should follow a methodical development process (see the Alles in Ordnung pattern, Section 3.1), such as the Unified Software Development Process [Jacobson 99]. A framework goes though each of the stages of methodical software development and will likely require more iterations than an equivalent application development effort.

The first key to successfully developing a framework is deciding what domain (functional models and processes) or domains you want to address and, within that, what applications you want to address. You can say you want a framework that addresses all applications in all domains, but be careful—if you take on too much, you will end up with requirements like "be able to write any business application," which quickly leads you to developing a programming language or a class library. These have value, but to be a framework, or at least a framework of value, the framework needs to be more focused. What about component frameworks like Java 2 Platform Enterprise Edition (J2EE)? Aren't they focused on being able to write any business application? Although they appear to be broadly applicable, these frameworks are actually narrowly targeted and support a specific domain, namely, the domain of distributed software component management.

A factor here is how much time you want to (or can) spend gathering the requirements. In order to develop a framework that addresses a set of applications in a domain (or domains), you need to have requirements from each of these applications (for each domain). Requirements are best gained from experts in the domain, for example, from business analysts for business applications. These domain experts do not have to be technically savvy—that is your technical team's job—but they need to know the applications (or more specifically, the business processes) in the domain (or domains) very well. This is unique to business application frameworks since, when developing most technical frameworks, the developer knows enough (or can quickly learn) about the domain. For example, with our prior engineering experience we could develop a device-management framework, however, we could not develop an accounting application; to do this, we need accountants.

Your process artifacts will vary depending on the development process you use. When developing the IBM SanFrancisco frameworks, we followed a process similar to the Rational Unified Process (which didn't exist at the time). For our process the deliverables were

- Requirements—a business-level description of what the framework does (what it does, not how it does it)
- Use cases—the business processes and tasks used to fulfill the requirements
- Analysis model—the business-level breakdown of the solution into business objects
- Design model—the design-level breakdown of the solution into classes
- Source code—the implementation
- Test cases—including both the business-level description and the code to test the framework code

Each of these artifacts was developed in an iterative fashion. Figure 1.1 shows how they relate to one another and who (technical versus domain experts) is responsible for them.

These and other deliverables are discussed in detail as part of the Unified Software Development Process [Jacobson 99] and in Appendix B.

An area that becomes challenging in business application or framework development is the split between domain and technical expertise. This split (having two people or groups of people own some of the artifacts) provides two challenges: (1) initially developing the artifacts, since each group will need to participate, and (2) keeping the related artifacts coherent with one

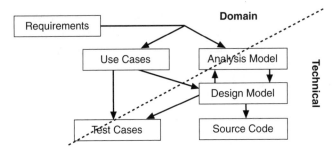

Figure 1.1 *How deliverables relate to one another and who owns them*

another during development iterations. To address these two challenges we add distinct points of contact between the domain and technical teams.

- Use case handoff—the completed requirements, use cases, and first-pass analysis model are given to the technical team by the domain team. The purpose of this meeting is for the members of the domain team to educate the technical team members so they can begin the design. At this point the technical team works with the domain team to refine the analysis model and begin producing the design model.

- Combined review—the domain and technical teams review a package consisting of the requirements, use cases, analysis model, design model, and test case definitions. This is to ensure that all of these deliverables are consistent before code development begins. The test cases are usually defined by the domain team from the use cases and then implemented by the technical team.

Within our process, these meetings form the minimum set of interactions the two teams can have.

These interaction points and the systematic development process into which they fit are critical for producing and keeping the artifacts consistent. Why should you care about keeping these internal artifacts consistent? Although they are internal when developing an application, they also become part of a framework's external deliverables.[1] If a framework provided only the code that implemented it, you would be able to map only above the code level once you did a lot of reverse engineering. The learning curve is big enough without that kind of obstacle! As discussed in the next section, the sooner the framework

---

1. Even if you are building an application, you'll be wise to develop and maintain these deliverables, since they will make application maintenance and enhancement much easier over time.

user can map to the framework, the greater the reuse. You want to create a framework that provides the pieces that allow users to map to it throughout the development process.

Another aspect of developing a framework is maintenance. Once the framework is developed, it will need to be maintained. The increased number of artifacts is both a blessing and a curse. It is a curse because you have more to maintain. You now have to consider sending out patches to your requirements, use cases, or models. This not only reduces user confusion but is also required by any tools that use this information. For example, a code generator that uses information in the design model to create the correct code depends on that model providing an accurate representation of the associated source code. It is a blessing because, especially when you provide the source code, it provides some of the benefits of open source software development. Your customers can provide their own patches and can send you their patches. This doesn't mean you have to accept their patches blindly, but it does give you a huge jump start in identifying and fixing problems.

1.4 Using Frameworks

When using a framework it is important to first ensure you get a framework that will give you the most reuse within your intended usage objectives. In other words, you want a framework that is well aligned with your needs. You don't want to spend all your time rewriting core elements of the framework— not only will you be getting very little value from the framework but you will also likely introduce difficult-to-debug errors because you don't understand all of the subtleties involved in the interaction between framework parts. In our planet example, if most of your planets have rings or moons, you probably don't want to use the framework we suggested in the example. As always, it is never that easy. Depending on how much effort you put into the development process, you might find a framework for creating arbitrary gravitational bodies that interact (planets, moons, comets, and so on) or discover a novel way to use our example framework to create two planets, one big and one small, and then place the smaller planet into orbit around the bigger one— voila, you now have a planet with a moon.

When looking for a framework to use, you have to realize that frameworks lie between two extremes: class libraries and applications. Although frameworks can be built on class libraries, they supply more than the class library's independent pieces, such as decimal support, time support, or a group of reusable collections. Frameworks that try to cover too much can become class libraries. And, even worse, these overextended frameworks can often create linkages between elements that make the frameworks difficult to use even as class libraries. On the other side of frameworks are applications. This is where frameworks that are too focused (that is, don't have enough extensibility) end up. This is not to say that any one of these solutions is better than another, only that you should pick the right one for your particular problem.

When should you use a framework? When you see the need to create a number of applications or a highly customizable application (because of the broad customer needs) in a particular domain (or domains) and you see that there is a common core of processes and functions, use a framework. The framework normally embodies the part you hate to reinvent every time you write that application, the part you hate to test every time, the part you would rather pay for once and never have to pay for again. Depending on the size and scope of this core, you'll use either a class library or a framework.

Once you've decided to use a framework and have found a suitable one, you need to integrate the use of the framework into your development process. Frameworks are more than pieces that can be reused when implementing your application. Depending on the scope of the framework, it may establish an underlying architecture to which you need to adhere.

A framework also provides a design for a solution to a domain process—such as a business process. You want to use these processes as soon as possible, taking advantage of the framework's work by reusing it. If you wait until you are implementing the code, you may be able to take advantage of certain pieces, but you won't get the greatest reuse—unless you come up with the same design, which is extremely unlikely. The best way to use a framework is to reuse it as soon as possible in your development process.

If you don't have a development process, it will be difficult if not impossible to use a framework. Our experience is that no matter what type of software you are developing, following some type of process, like the Unified Software Development Process [Jacobson 99] or the Extreme Programming (XP) process [Beck 00], greatly increases a project's chance for success.

The most effective way to use a framework is to add mapping steps to each step in your development process. This mapping involves stopping and taking a look at what the framework provides. If you are developing requirements, look for matching requirements. If you are designing your application, align your design with framework design elements. The key is that you must explicitly incorporate and enforce the mapping process—it is much too easy to skip the mapping step, especially if this is the first time using a framework. The most benefit is gained from a framework if you can map early (see the Map Early, Map Often pattern, Section 9.2). If you map at the requirements level, not only will you be able to reuse the use cases but also the analysis, design, implementation, and testing will have already been done for you. For example, if you are building currency conversion support into your application, your requirements are likely to include the abilities to convert currencies, to have the exchange rate vary daily, and to use different exchange rates for hard currency versus traveler's checks. In the IBM SanFrancisco framework [Monday 99], these requirements, stated more generically, are directly supported by the framework: establishing exchange rates via date or period and supporting exchange rate tables for whatever the user wants to define. We can map from those requirements to the framework requirements and start the reuse at this highest level.

While mapping is key to using a framework, it is also the bane of framework use. You need to know what there is to map to (see the Just Learn It pattern, Section 9.1). You are trying to deliver a product, so you don't have infinite time for the mapping stages. You map to what you know about and what you've discovered so far. How much time can you spend learning and discovering? You should spend as much time as you can up front—before you start using the framework. There's probably a core you have to learn (which the framework documentation should identify); after that you can grow your knowledge over time. Even if you don't understand the entire framework up front and you miss something you could have reused, you will still benefit from the things you did reuse.

You can also use a framework as an example. To support mapping, a framework should provide end-to-end documentation and development artifacts. This level of documentation, if done correctly, gives you, in essence, an in-depth case study of one way to approach a domain through all phases of development, including the patterns used as the framework was developed. Often these patterns can be used completely independently of the framework, especially if they have been truly captured as patterns.

1.5 The Framework Process Patterns

As discussed in the Preface, we've chosen to use a patterns-based approach in this book. We've further organized these patterns into seven distinct categories, each addressing a separate aspect of frameworks. Chapter 3 (the first chapter that presents the patterns) addresses patterns that are common across the entire development process. This includes architectural patterns as well. Chapters 4 through 7 describe patterns specific to individual artifacts from the development process: requirements, analysis, design, and documentation. Chapter 8 looks at the social aspects of creating a strong and focused development team. Finally, Chapter 9 explores how customers use the framework. Together these patterns cover all the factors (product, process, development team, and customer) that go into the development and use of a successful framework.

An alternative way of looking at these patterns is by the area (or discipline) that they address. In Table 1.1 (which is also printed on the inside back cover) we've categorized the patterns in each part by these areas:

- Communication—Information must be properly communicated.
- Consistency—The same things should be done the same way.
- Iteration—Software development involves iteration, and frameworks are no exception. In fact, for frameworks there is unique iteration related to refining them to their target applications in their target domain.
- Incompleteness—Sometimes you should leave a framework incomplete so that framework users have the ability to complete (extend) it to their particular needs.
- Flexibility—You need to determine how much extensibility a framework should support and where it should support it.
- Duh—Some things are obvious but still can cause problems if you aren't careful.

These patterns will be demonstrated through the use of a case study, presented in Chapter 2.

Table 1.1 *Patterns Presented in This Book*

Patterns and Their Locations

Pattern Category	Development Process (Chapter 3)	Requirements (Chapter 4)	Analysis (Chapter 5)	Design (Chapter 6)	Documentation (Chapter 7)	Social Aspects (Chapter 8)	Framework Use (Chapter 9)
Communication	Alles in Ordnung (20) Innocent Questions (29) Divide and Conquer (35) Exposing It All (52)		Eating the Elephant (88) Where's Mr. Spock When You Need Him? (102)		Souvenirs (140) Give 'Em What They Want (145)	The Great Communicator (160)	Just Learn It (176)
Iteration	Iterate, Iterate, Iterate (46)		Eating the Elephant (88) Something Is Better Than Nothing (97)	Missed It by That Much (116)			Map Early, Map Often (181)
Consistency	Consistency Is King (40)			Missed It by That Much (116) That's the Way the Cookie Crumbles (127)		Consistency Czar (165)	
Incompleteness		Tor's Second Cousin (67) The Stupid Test (81)		Pass the Buck (110)			
Flexibility	Innocent Questions (29)	It Depends (62) What, Not How (75)					
"Duh"				It's Still OO to Me (132)		There Is No "I" in Team (154)	Color Inside the Lines (185)

Chapter
2

Case Study

In this case study we define a neutral domain and a set of requirements for that domain. This provides a common basis from which we can explore and provide examples for each of the patterns. This neutral domain needs to have the characteristics of a business domain so that we can explore some of the unique situations, such as the split between domain and technical knowledge, that occur when developing application frameworks. It needs to be a neutral domain so that we can focus on the problems specific to frameworks and not to a particular domain. All nonfrivolous domains bring lots of baggage with them. This baggage consists of issues and practices that usually take years for experts to grasp. If we were to pick any specific, existing domain, we would have to either spend many pages teaching you the domain or ignore those important issues—much to the frustration of anyone familiar with that domain. Instead, we have picked a "frivolous" domain that we believe everyone can quickly understand and that still allows us to demonstrate and focus on the issues of developing a framework and not of a particular domain.

2.1 The Clothing Management Domain

We've chosen the family of clothing management applications from the near future as our domain. These future applications will take over the tedious task of selecting clothing to wear, keeping it clean and repaired, and replacing it when worn out or obsolete. This domain is one that everyone should understand. We all deal with clothing. Whether it's fig leaves, togas, or blue jeans, we all manage clothes in one form or another.

Your first response may be that this isn't an interesting problem because it isn't complex enough—it is easy for you to do these things. If you are looking at one particular set of requirements, we agree. However, we need to create a framework from which we can fulfill many different sets of requirements, building applications for a variety of individuals. For example, one individual might have a very limited set of clothing (such as seven identical sets of clothing, one for each day of the week), so they need only a simple application. However, fashion models need a much more complex application since they always have to look their best—their jobs depend on it. Our framework needs to be able to support building either of these applications.

This case study focuses on requirements. The individual patterns use these requirements as a starting point for their examples and approaches.

2.2 Overview

After domain analysis and requirements refinement is completed, the following requirements are identified in the clothing management domain.

1. **Selecting**—deciding what to wear
   a. How you select clothing changes based on what you are going to do in it.
   b. Appropriateness must be checked for articles selected to be worn together.
   c. The cleanliness of an article of clothing can impact whether or not it is selected.
   d. The state of repair of an article of clothing can impact whether or not it is selected.
   e. The environment in which you plan to wear the clothing can impact the selection.
2. **Cleaning**—handling the dirty laundry
   a. Determining when an article needs to be cleaned must be customizable.
   b. For each article of clothing the cleaning method should be able to be specified.

3. **Repairing**—fixing damaged clothing
   a. Determining when an article of clothing needs to be repaired must be customizable.
   b. A process with specific customizable steps needs to be supported for deciding on and initiating repairs.
4. **Purchasing**—getting additional clothing
   a. A customizable frequency of clothing purchase and the criteria used for determining what clothing to buy must be provided.
   b. Different modes of clothing purchase need to be supported.

Let's look at each of these in more detail.

2.3 Selecting Clothing

Most people don't just pick whatever clothing they happen to come across. What factors go into selecting the right clothing? We can't address all aspects here, but we can look at enough situations to make the requirements for our framework interesting and to induce the problems that will allow us to explore the patterns.

- **What are you going to do in the clothing?** If you're going to your job as a Las Vegas blackjack dealer, you'll want (and need) different clothing than if you're going to your job as a cowboy. Otherwise when you show up dressed as a blackjack dealer at your cowboy job, you'll find that the clothing will be ruined (or destroyed) since it is not made to handle the rigors of being a cowboy. Likewise, if you show up to your blackjack dealer job dressed as a cowboy, people will be surprised and confused when you look different from all the other blackjack dealers. The requirement is that you be able to change how you select clothing based on what you are going to do in it.

- **Is each article of clothing appropriate with the others?** If you're wearing a swimsuit on your lower body, you wouldn't normally select a dress shirt, tie, and jacket for your upper body. In addition to this obvious problem, there are more subtle problems, such as wearing an orange-red shirt with pink-red pants. However, if our system is to be used by circus clowns, the definition of appropriateness is different—if clothing clashes, it's appropriate. The requirement is that you be able to check the appropriateness of the articles being selected to be worn together.

- **How clean is the clothing?** When making repairs on a truck, you know you're going to get messy, so you might choose to wear clothing that isn't clean—especially if the only other option is a white dress shirt. The requirement is that the cleanliness of the clothing can be considered as part of making the selection.

- **Does the clothing need repair?** If you've ever split a pair of pants or had an unfortunate rip in an article of clothing, you don't usually want to wear it again until it is repaired. So, just like cleanliness, the state of repair (or need of repair) can be a factor. However, this also isn't that simple. A past trend among teenagers was to rip out the knees on a pair of jeans. This takes an ordinary pair of jeans and makes them much "cooler," but it doesn't mean they need repair. The requirement here is that the state of repair of the clothing can be used as part of making the selection.

- **In what environment are you wearing the clothing?** In some parts of Europe, the accepted norm for clothing seems to be much more formal than in the United States. For example, a bright purple coat would stand out among the mainly dark brown and black coats. So, depending on whether or not you want to stand out, you could use either European selection criteria or U.S. selection criteria. Other cultural differences, too numerous to list, can impact this and have disastrous results—such as a woman wearing a bikini in Saudi Arabia. The requirement is that the environment in which you plan to wear the clothing can impact making the selection.

2.4 Cleaning Clothing

- **How often do you clean it?** It might be after two hours of use or it might be never. For normal use of the article a means of determining when it should be cleaned is needed. Frequency of cleaning depends on many factors: cultural, personal, professional, and characteristics of the item itself. A doctor has to wear clean scrubs. However, a scarf or tie can be worn several times before it needs to be cleaned. The requirement is that determining when an article needs to be cleaned must be customizable.

- **How should it be cleaned?** Once you've decided that an article needs to be cleaned you need to determine how it should be cleaned. Incorrect washing can be disastrous. For example, washing a cashmere sweater in the washing machine will probably ruin it. For the purposes of this case study, we're going to assume there are only a few fixed ways to clean an item (wash and dry clean) and the only customization needed is the ability to specify which of these is appropriate for a particular article of clothing. The requirement is that you need to be able to specify the cleaning method on each article of clothing.

2.5 Repairing Clothing

- **Is it damaged?** Determining whether something needs repair is similar to determining selection and cleanliness. The criteria must be flexible because we don't know when something will be damaged or if it was damaged on purpose. How the article is used can impact the decision. For example, a missing top button doesn't prevent wearing a shirt on which you never button the top button. The requirement is that determining when an article of clothing needs to be repaired must be customizable.

- **How and when should it be repaired?** Once you've determined that you need to repair an article of clothing, you have to determine how you are going to repair it. There will be limitations based on the article of clothing. For example, using duct tape to repair a tear in a business suit is unacceptable, whereas it is perfectly fine for a "work on the car" sweatshirt—possibly preferable because you have duct tape easily available for fixing the car. You also have to look at the abilities and time you have for making repairs. You might not have a sewing machine or even the ability to sew. Finally, you have to decide whether it is worth making the repair. If it costs less to buy a new item, you probably shouldn't make the repair. In other words, you need to determine what kind of repairs are needed, determine how they need to get done, evaluate whether it is worth making them, and then initiate the repair. The requirement is that a process with specific customizable steps needs to be supported for deciding on and initiating repairs.

2.6 Purchasing Clothing

- **When should new clothing be purchased?** Many factors can affect clothing purchase, including available budget, the state of wear of the current wardrobe, the need to stay in fashion, and the availability of time to consider potential purchases. The framework needs to allow you to incorporate any or all of these factors into the purchasing algorithm in varying degrees and should also allow you to add your own criteria. The requirement is that a customizable frequency of clothing purchase and the criteria used for determining what clothing to buy must be provided.

- **Where can I purchase clothing?** Framework users may want to be able to include many purchase options in their application, including retail stores, mail order catalogs, Web-based purchasing, and perhaps even personal shoppers and hand-tailored clothing. The requirement is that different modes of clothing purchase need to be supported.

Although this list of requirements could be much longer, these situations are enough to allow us to meaningfully examine the problem of providing a framework that allows applications that fulfill these requirements to be built.

Chapter

3

The Development Process

Although many of the patterns in this book relate to the individual steps in the development process, there are a number of patterns that apply across the entire process. These patterns have to do with the overall architecture of the framework and things to consider when selecting and executing the framework development process. These patterns include

- Alles in Ordnung (Section 3.1)—using a methodical development process to keep framework development on track

- Innocent Questions (Section 3.2)—connecting the domain and technical experts so that knowledge doesn't get missed or unspoken

- Divide and Conquer (Section 3.3)—making the framework consumable by decomposing the framework into large, interrelated pieces

- Consistency Is King (Section 3.4)—maintaining consistency throughout the framework

- Iterate, Iterate, Iterate (Section 3.5)—recognizing the importance of refinement iteration and how to make sure it takes only three iterations, at most, to get it right

- Exposing It All (Section 3.6)—realizing that the framework's customers are the framework's partners and thus need more information than they would for other types of software

These six patterns are discussed in detail in this chapter.

3.1 Alles in Ordnung[1]

Also Known As

Follow a Methodical Development Process

Intent

Although any software development project can benefit from following a methodical development process, such a process is essential to building a successful framework. This doesn't have to be an overbearing monster of a process. It can be any process that allows you to consistently create the artifacts the framework consumer needs.

Context

Remember when you were writing a program for a class assignment. If your classes were anything like ours, the professor didn't care how the program looked or how it performed, as long as it got the right result. Although we can argue the merits of this teaching methodology, this *laissez-faire* approach often gets carried over into the working world. As long as the program fulfills the requirements, no one cares what's inside.

Everything is wonderful until the first change in requirements. Now you have to make a change to what you wrote (or, if you're lucky, maintenance is someone else's problem). How do you figure out what to change and how to change it? There are lots of solutions to this problem, and object-oriented framework techniques are among the many proposed solutions. However, not all object-oriented software is created equal. Which would you rather change?

- Code that follows standards and has a well-documented set of requirements, a well-documented design, and good interface documentation and code comments. Let's even throw in automated self-checking test cases that verify adherence to the requirements.
- A blob of code hacked out in a caffeine-induced trance. The requirements were on the back of an envelope, the design was (and may still be) on the whiteboard in the developer's office, code comments are in a foreign language—one that can be understood only when under the influence of large doses of caffeine—and test cases consisted of doing "stuff" until the code didn't break anymore.

---

1. German for "All Is in Order."

The second situation is a programmer's worst nightmare (and also makes most managers lose sleep at night). Usually you won't encounter all of these events together, but you will encounter many of them individually. For example, we've had responsibility for maintaining code that existed only as compiled machine instructions and a printout. The source code had been lost years before. All the help the senior programmers could give us was to say that the code worked and we probably shouldn't touch it.

Does this mean that you have to have a heavyweight process that you follow before you can develop any software? Definitely not! Regardless of the implications of this chapter's title, we aren't trying to get you to swallow lots of process (or any particular process). The title sounds more severe than it really is—from a German perspective, when all is in order, life is operating smoothly and predictably. Software can be successfully developed without a methodical development process; however, its chances of success are greatly reduced.

Framework development, on the other hand, cannot succeed without a methodical development process. A framework doesn't have the luxury of providing just code that works. More artifacts than you expect (discussed in the Exposing It All pattern, Section 3.6) need to be produced and provided in a way that enables framework users to map to the framework (see the Map Early, Map Often pattern, Section 9.2). This consistent set of navigable artifacts won't happen by accident. More importantly, framework users (your partners) are not as forgiving as application users.

If you don't have a development process, the resulting anarchy creates a jumbled mass of unrelated and inconsistent artifacts that framework users must wade through before they can use the framework. The cognitive dissonance, as discussed in the Consistency Is King pattern (see Section 3.4), becomes too much for framework users to overcome. The framework users want to learn something (at whatever level) once and then be able to leverage that knowledge in another part of the framework. The end result without a development process is that the users discard the framework and are then accused of having "not invented here" syndrome.[2]

---

2. We feel that there are two aspects of what is called the "not invented here" syndrome. One is based on its origins—developers who don't want to reuse anything from anyone else. The other is based on developers who want to reuse but are unable to—no matter how hard they try, the software they are trying to reuse just isn't reusable. The difficulty as a technical leader is to discern which situation is occurring so you can break through the first and support the second.

Example

If we aren't following a methodical development process, we can easily end up with different solutions for the same problem. Looking at a portion of the clothing framework development, this could happen when working on the selection and repair portions of the framework.

When developing the clothing selection portion of the framework, let's assume we decided to follow the Strategy design pattern[3] and encapsulated the selection in a strategy object. As shown in Figure 3.1, we provided a Person class with a select method on it. The select method locates the strategy object (the specific subclass of the SelectStrategy abstract class with which it was configured) and delegates the request to it. We used the Strategy design pattern because our documented requirements indicated this algorithm was volatile.

In the case of the repair portion of the framework, our requirements came from talking to the domain experts over lunch. We remembered that the volatility of the repair requirements are such that this portion of the framework doesn't need the flexibility of the Strategy design pattern. Thus we simply coded the algorithm that sends the item to the tailor directly in the body of the repair method defined by the ClothingItem.

Once developed, we shipped the framework with interface documentation only. None of the other artifacts (including the diagram in Figure 3.1) were part of the process, so being efficient programmers we either didn't create them or didn't bother keeping them around when we did.

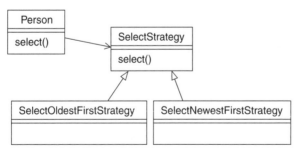

Figure 3.1   *Strategy pattern example*

---

3. The Strategy design pattern involves encapsulating an algorithm in a separate strategy object so that the algorithm can be modified (by changing between members of the strategy object's subclasses) without impact on the original class [Gamma 94].

Now let's look at this example from the perspective of someone trying to use the framework. Because of the missing artifacts our domain experts can't map our requirements to the requirements fulfilled by the framework. They have to either look at the code (which domain experts may not be able to do) or guess. How they guess is based on their experience with the framework. For the selection portion of the framework, they guess that flexibility is there, and they are right. However, when they come to the repair portion, flexibility isn't there. If they encounter the portions in this order, they get in trouble the second time they make the assumption, which means they will probably never assume it again.[4] If, on the other hand, they encounter the repair portion first, they will find the simple class implementation and are likely to assume the same for the selection portion, thus missing the framework support. In the extreme, they might even decide not to use the framework because they assume it doesn't have the flexibility they need.

A similar thing happens at the lower levels of the framework. At the design level, encountering the strategy object in the first case and not in the second makes users wonder why the strategy object isn't there—possibly making them question their understanding. Or they might first encounter the case without the strategy object, in which event they may not know to look for the Strategy design pattern in the second case, causing them to replace the entire class instead of taking advantage of the provided flexibility. If they'd had the higher-level artifacts they'd have been able to tell that we'd thought the flexibility wasn't needed in the one case—and, during development, we would have had the opportunity to evaluate this decision more formally to ensure it was correct.

As this example shows, consistency (as discussed in the Consistency Is King pattern, Section 3.4) is important across all framework artifacts. Keeping all the artifacts consistent makes them much easier to use and understand. Without a methodical development process, keeping this consistency would be difficult, if not impossible.

If we now look at the example from the perspective of the framework maintainer we have a different problem. The missing artifacts make it almost impossible to make changes with confidence. We've been getting comments from the customers that the repair support isn't flexible enough. Were the

---

4. Remember the first time you touched a burner on a stove? An adult was probably around so it was turned off and it wasn't all that interesting. Sometime later you touched it when it was on. We'll bet you didn't touch it again, at least for a long, long time. Burning a framework user achieves the same result.

requirements incorrect or were they misunderstood? Or were they understood and there were compelling reasons for not using a flexible design solution? Hopefully someone who was there when the framework was created is around; otherwise, there isn't any way to tell. This is another place where a methodical development process can help. When the developers follow a process and capture the appropriate artifacts, it is more likely that the reasons for their choices will be documented as part of one of the artifacts. While this is important, it isn't a silver bullet. Even with a methodical development process producing good artifacts, some information will fall through the cracks. A choice will be made that is fundamental, so fundamental that once it is made no one would think to write it down. These are the things that are in people's heads and usually are recognized and captured only over time.

Inconsistencies and missing artifacts are like trying to understand a piece of modern art: you often have to guess what the original intent was. Have you ever read the title just to get a clue? Sometimes users of your framework will be able to figure out your intent, but do you want to bet your framework on it?

Problem

A framework is much more than application programming interfaces. It is a set of top-to-bottom artifacts that allows the framework user to effectively and efficiently identify reusable assets and map to the framework. Inconsistent artifacts increase the cognitive dissonance and thus lower the likelihood the framework will be used—and used effectively. Missing artifacts leave the framework user guessing about the intent.

Approaches

There are many different approaches to solving this problem (and they are also discussed in other patterns), but the key is that in order to use those approaches, you need a consistent development process on which to hang them.

Two extreme approaches to process are anarchy (in other words, lack of any process) and a rigid, heavyweight, "no wiggle room" process. Let's first look at these two and then look at a more realistic approach.

Anarchy (or lack of process), although a common initial approach, really won't help ensure you get a usable framework. It might happen by accident, but that is about as likely as a room full of monkeys with typewriters producing the first act of Hamlet. This freestyle approach has one (and only one) advantage: it requires no education of the team. It doesn't need to be monitored since there are two states, "working on it" and "done." Coming out of college, this is often the programmer's view of the world. On the other hand, this is the project manager's nightmare: he or she doesn't know if the software will make it until it's done—or the deadline passes. Too often, when left alone, this is how programmers run software development.

On the other end of the spectrum is a process that makes a hyperactive project manager smile. Taken to absurdity, every action including going to the toilet and taking a break to get a drink is tracked by the schedule. At any second, the manager can tell if the project is on schedule or not. Usually the project isn't on schedule because people are spending so much time providing data for tracking reports, discussing status, and otherwise feeding the process animal that they aren't getting much "real work" done. In this extreme case, nirvana has been reached since there are even processes for the processes! Everything is documented and the team has meetings about how the average toilet use time is not within the expected bounds of the schedule. The advantage of this process is that it makes sure nothing is missed. No item slips through. What comes out is nearly perfect. The disadvantage is that by the time the mandatory four years of process education are completed, the process has changed, so you have to start again. Also, too much time is spent on the care and feeding of the process rather than producing code. This environment drives programmers crazy. All too often, this is how managers run software development.

Our experience is that—in spite of themselves—either of these methods can work (not necessarily delivering quality code on time and under budget, but eventually something will get out the door through sheer effort and individual heroics). However, neither method is optimal for software development. The right place is somewhere in between, what Alistair Cockburn refers to as "Big-M Methodology" [Cockburn 98, p. 78]—that place where there's just enough process to make sure we stay on track and not so much that all we do is process. Have we found this utopia? Sadly, we don't think it exists. What exists is a range of options that are all correct; you just have to pick what is right for you. These are the in-between points where your project can succeed. This is often how engineers run software development.

Besides hiring engineers to run your software development, how can you find out what's right for you? Although each case is unique, we've identified a few rules of thumb that have helped us.

Start with an Existing Process

If you already have a process that works, start with it. If you don't have an existing process, look at something like the Unified Software Development

Process [Jacobson 99] or Extreme Programming process [Beck 00]. It is always easier (and more successful) to document the differences from an already described process than to define a process from scratch. This allows you to take advantage of the existing documentation and education for that process, rather than having to create your own.

This isn't to say you should teach a cat to love water. If there really isn't another way, create your own process (although you should think at least twice before setting off down this road—existing processes are quite flexible and effective). If you do, make sure you document the process well and make sure all your developers understand what it is and what they are supposed to do.

One way to evaluate and work with a process is provided by the Capability Maturity Model [Carnegie Mellon 02], which describes five levels of process. For example, the anarchy situation mentioned above is the first level, Initial, which is an ad hoc and chaotic process whose success is based on individual heroics and effort.

Look at the Artifacts That Are Parts of Your Product

These won't be the same from product to product; the Exposing It All pattern (see Section 3.6) describes how we've done this for frameworks. If you have to ship an artifact as part of the product, it should probably be the result of part of your process. This means you should identify when that artifact is created and how it is kept up-to-date.

Understand When Knowledge Transfers

Where does knowledge transfer from one group or team to another? In our case when we went from the requirements and scenarios to the design we changed from a team of domain experts to a team of object-oriented design experts. We had to have artifacts to capture and transfer this knowledge. The information we captured and the transition process is discussed in the Innocent Questions pattern (see Section 3.2).

Look for Special Events in the Development Process

Look for places where going back would be painful and places where convergence is critical. In our case, just before coding we wanted the design to be as complete and stable as possible. To achieve this we added a process step called the *combined review*. In this review all of the domain and design artifacts were reviewed as a whole to ensure the design's completeness, consistency, and accuracy in meeting the requirements. In this key review, both the domain and design teams participated, including the domain lead and design lead.

Don't Throw Out Project Management

Reducing the project management overhead while still keeping the ability to manage the project is a tedious balancing act. Even the anarchy described earlier in this chapter is more appealing than being in a process with the wrong project management points. These erroneous points will irritate both the programmer and the manager. The programmer is not motivated to feed the process, and when he or she does, the manager can't really tell whether or not the project is on track. Returning to our absurd example, the process includes steps to record every time a developer uses the toilet. Our empirical data show that the closer programmers are to being done with the software, the less often they use the toilet. Thus, we can graph toilet usage and when it reaches zero, our project is done. With this process, the programmers now complain about tracking every time they go to the toilet, and their managers have to watch for people not entering their toilet usage correctly. Upper management, in sheer horror of a recent meteoric rise in usage, delays the announcement of the product—not realizing that the results may be a result of an outbreak of flu among the group.

Clearly this is an absurd example, but we've seen processes that track things that made almost as little sense. While you want to avoid onerous processes, don't think that you have to get your process right the first time. As with any successful process, you have to be flexible and adapt. In our toilet usage example, had management looked more carefully at the *influ*enced data, they might have changed what was measured, or at least tempered their response.

Solution

- Use a methodical development process.
- Find a balance between anarchy and tight-fisted order.
- If possible, start from an existing process.
- Leverage experience, existing documentation, and existing education.
- Determine what artifacts your process should produce based on product needs.
- Determine when knowledge is transferred.
- Look for special events in the development process.
- Don't throw out project management—instead, find a balance.

When to Use/Not Use

If you have a process that you already love and use—and it works (an important and often overlooked point)—don't throw it out. If it isn't already a framework development process, you probably should review it to see what, if any, tweaks need to be made to support the development of frameworks.

If you have to come up with a process, don't start from an existing process if it really doesn't fit. If there isn't an existing process you can use, then go ahead and create your own (but before you do this, be very sure that you can't reuse or adapt an existing process). Given the extensive writings on the topic of software development over the past few years, we'd be very surprised if you can't find a well-documented process that can serve as your starting point.

Don't use this rule expecting to get your process right the first time. You have to do your best with the best information available at the time and then, as new information becomes available or the situation changes, you have to adapt your process. Never forget that the process is there to help both programmers and project managers. Contrary to popular opinion, these two groups are not mortal enemies—at least they shouldn't be since a good project manager can help programmers focus on what needs to get done at the right time in the development cycle. The key point here is if an element of the process stops being beneficial, it should be changed.

Don't be tricked into believing that having a good process (or any process for that matter) guarantees the success of your project. For framework development a good process is necessary but not sufficient for success. For example, in addition to a good process it is crucial to ensure you are addressing the right requirements (see It Depends, Section 4.1) and that your framework can be consumed (see Consistency Is King, Section 3.4; Exposing It All, Section 3.6; and Give 'Em What They Want, Section 7.2).

Applicability

- Don't throw away a process that works.
- Try to use an existing process, but don't force it to fit.
- Process definition is an iterative process.
- Having a process isn't enough to guarantee success.

Known Uses

The fact that process is a key ingredient to effective software development has become a more widespread belief in the software community. Once we were out of college, all of the projects we've worked on have had some type of process. We've worked under a tight-fisted process and more recently under more balanced processes. We've worked with others who've used little or no process.

When we began working on the IBM SanFrancisco project we recognized that the existing processes were inadequate (this was prior to documentation of the Unified Software Development Process and the Extreme Programming process) and would require too much modification to be practical. Based on our process experience and industry practices at the time, we defined an initial framework development process. As we developed the framework we refined this initial process to the process outlined in Appendix B. These refinements came as we learned the lessons captured as patterns in this book and as the development team grew. If we were starting over, we would use the process we ended up with as a guideline for how to modify one of the more broadly known processes.

Related Patterns

- Innocent Questions (Section 3.2)—using artifacts enables communication that will help define your development process.
- Consistency Is King (Section 3.4)—a methodical development process is key to consistency.
- Exposing It All (Section 3.6)—using the artifacts that will be given to the customer helps define your development process.

3.2 Innocent Questions

Also Known As

Connecting Domain and Technical Experts

Intent

As software moves into the business application realm and as technologies continue their rapid advance, it becomes more and more rare for one person to have both the necessary domain and technical expertise. Improving the connection between experts greatly improves the software they produce.

Context

In the good old days of software development, the problems solved with software were mainly ones for which the same person was both the technical expert and the domain expert. Now the few people who fit this criteria, especially those who know the latest technology and a "hot" domain, are worth their weight in gold. These are the people who swoop in, immediately see the fatal flaw, and, with one sentence, destroy a technical design or a business requirement. These experts are simultaneously hated and worshiped. If you've got one of these on your team, don't let him or her go. If you don't have enough of these people (which you won't), you'll have situations where one person is a domain expert and another is a technical expert.

With the right mix of domain and technical experts, there usually won't be any problems. They will regulate themselves and create a successful and beneficial collaboration. Unfortunately, finding people who can easily work in such collaborations is also difficult. Practices need to be established that allow people with less than optimal combinations of domain and technical skills to work effectively together.

Example

To develop the repair portion of the clothing framework, we pair together a senior tailor and a new computer science graduate. The senior tailor, in our example, is very set in his ways. There is one way to repair items and only one way—at least that's how he appears on the surface. It turns out that if you acknowledge his expertise as a tailor, he is very receptive to making sure that the requirements and use cases support the more general goals of the framework. Unfortunately our recent graduate has minimal people skills and is intolerant of anyone who isn't into technology. Ask him a technical question and his single-syllable answers and attitude can lead to implications of stupidity. This team is very unlikely to succeed.

On the other hand, the selection team consists of an experienced dresser who has dressed models and actors and an experienced object-oriented designer who has done lots of design and even led development teams. Both are good with people and receptive to questions and criticism. This team is very likely to succeed.

Unfortunately having any one of our teams fail may mean that the entire project fails. We need all the teams to succeed or at least have the best possibility of success we can achieve with the people we've got.

Problem

How do we increase the likelihood that all our mixed development teams will succeed?

Approaches

There are a number of ways to approach this problem. One is to rearrange the teams to avoid the extreme of our clothing repair team. We probably can't, or shouldn't, change the domain expert. It was difficult to attract an experienced tailor to the team. Even though developers are also in short supply, in comparison to tailors, we have lots of object-oriented developers. In this case, their expertise is probably reasonably interchangeable.[5] In this example, we can move the new object-oriented developer from our repair team to the selection team and transfer the experienced developer to the repair team. Although this makes what appears to be two weaker teams, it strengthens the overall development team by making it much more likely both will succeed. Unfortunately you can't always foresee these situations when setting up the teams initially, and sometimes rearranging teams can become messy—someone might want to know why he or she is being reassigned.

If we can't rearrange the teams, what can we do to help encourage the teams to be more effective? One approach is to ensure that the team members understand their roles and what is expected of them in those roles. This sounds simple, but we've found that explicitly stating that one is the domain expert and the other the technical expert helps. This includes identifying clear responsibility for the different framework artifacts or facets of those artifacts. For example, for our original repair team, the tailor is responsible for the requirements and the use cases for the framework and the developer is responsible for the design and code. This doesn't mean the developer gets to sit on his hands during the requirements and use case phases. He is responsible for asking questions about the requirements and use cases. Thus when the requirements from the tailor don't include iron-on patches, the developer can ask the innocent question about why they aren't included. Similarly during design the tailor should ask how certain requirements are being filled, especially at extension points. We've found this explicit distinction works because it makes clear up front who is the expert at each point and that it is the other's job to ask the innocent questions—and they are doing it to help each other, not to annoy, irritate, or enrage their working partner.

To ensure that good communication occurred throughout the development process we used for the IBM SanFrancisco project (see Appendix B), we also established well-defined checkpoints when a team developing a specific feature had to interact with the broader development team. In particular we

---

5. This is not a license to get "programmer object" syndrome. In this syndrome all programmers are treated as interchangeable objects because they are all instances of the programmer base class.

identified two checkpoints that each piece of the framework had to go through. These were the *requirements handoff* and the *combined review.*

The requirements handoff checkpoint occurs when the requirements and use cases are at a point that a rudimentary analysis object model is in place and design can begin. This varies in completeness of requirements, use cases, and models from team to team, but it is the point at which the main focus changes from the domain person's deliverables to the developer's deliverables. The domain lead and technical lead usually both participate in this review. The domain lead's primary job is to validate the requirements, use cases, and domain content of the analysis model, and the technical lead focuses on suggesting design approaches the developer should consider that become evident as the models and other documentation are being discussed (for example, suggesting patterns that should be considered). This meeting is typically an educational meeting with the domain person explaining the requirements and use cases and the other participants asking questions. If you are one of the leads, this checkpoint allows you to observe the team and decide whether team dynamics are a problem. This checkpoint represents a large educational investment by the developer, so once this meeting has occurred, you shouldn't recommend rearranging the team. At this point, style differences and interteam problems should be treated using techniques that are beyond the scope of this book.

The combined review checkpoint occurs when coding is ready to start. At this checkpoint the requirements, use cases, and design models should be completed. The focus of this review is to validate that the pieces match one another and that the design correctly reflects the requirements and use cases. Both leads must be involved in this checkpoint. The goal is to eliminate or at least minimize changes once coding starts.

These are the key checkpoints you must incorporate into the process when developing frameworks. They provide not only timely feedback but also a minimum number of places where the technical and domain teams must interact. However, these two checkpoints should never be taken as the only places the teams are allowed to interact—we encourage constant interaction between technical and domain team members throughout the development cycle. Ideally members responsible for the same features share an office or at least are located close to one another. The more interaction or opportunity for interaction between the two halves, the better. This includes interaction with the leads. The leads must be available and must continually check with and work with the teams, often leading by example by asking the innocent questions.

Another way to make the team work better is by improving the proximity of the team members. Ideally, as mentioned above, having them share an office or at least sit near one another is simple and very effective. For example, when working on the IBM SanFrancisco project, we were very cautious about having a domain person in Stockholm, Sweden, and a developer seven time zones away in Rochester, Minnesota. We have seen similar situations work, but usually when the two people had previously worked together at the same location. If they cannot be together, it is crucial to get face-to-face time between the team members at the beginning of the project. We've observed during a number of phone conferences that when the person on the phone has had face-to-face time with the people in the room, they give him or her the benefit of the doubt—especially when something negative or questionable is said. On the other hand, the people in the room are quick to take offense to a similar comment by a person with whom they've had little or no face-to-face time. There are many other ways to make distributed development effective, but capturing our experience in making effective distributed teams is beyond the scope of this book.

No matter what you do some teams will have problems and others will excel. We've been lucky to have really good people on our teams; they have been able to work through the rough spots. As in most cases, having intelligent, motivated, charismatic people with good senses of humor is not a necessity, but it certainly helps. Luckily success doesn't require perfect people.

Solution

- Try to form development teams with people who are compatible.
- Clearly define roles and ownership.
  - Ask innocent questions.
  - Keep your sense of humor.
- Have well-defined, required interaction points.
  - Emphasize that these provide the *minimum* amount of interaction between the teams.
- Keep the team in close proximity.
  - Get face-to-face time for distributed teams—especially when first forming them.
- Hire good people—they will make it work.

When to Use/Not Use

As with anything involving people, this pattern must be adapted to your particular situation. If you blindly apply this rule, you could get catastrophic results. For example, if you rearrange the repair team at the combined review checkpoint, the tailor will be angry because he has to redo the domain education and the developer will be angry because he was just about to get to code, which he anticipated like the pot of gold at the end of the design rainbow. In addition, how will you respond to the "why" questions—"Why did you rearrange the teams?" You probably don't want to have to say, "Because you're impossible to work with." This might not make things better. You can always try feeding the person's ego: "Your expertise is really needed over here." Again this can backfire when the person finds out his or her job on the new team is minor.

Don't feel like you have to do something. If the teams are working, leave them alone. Too often trying to make the teams perfect makes things worse rather than better.

Applicability

- Your particular situation will be unique.
- Leave teams that are working well alone—trying to make them better may actually break them.

Known Uses

We've used variations of this pattern throughout our careers. Anytime more than two people are involved team dynamics will be an issue. When we were developing the IBM SanFrancisco frameworks, especially since they were application frameworks, we found that the separation of domain and technical expertise and the differences in those experts' backgrounds made the recognition and management of these team dynamics critical to the project's success.

Related Pattern

- Alles in Ordnung (Section 3.1)—well-defined interaction points are needed in the development process.

3.3 Divide and Conquer

Also Known As

Making the Framework Consumable

Intent

Unless you and your customer have lots of big-brained people,[6] you need to divide the framework (or any other large piece of software) into pieces that make it easier to develop and easier to consume.

Context

Do you have lots of big-brained people on your development team? Does your customer? The answer is probably no. These people are few and far between—and usually expensive to hire and retain. How do we make sure that our development team and the customers using the framework can be effective without requiring big-brained people?

One of the strengths a big-brained person brings to a project is the ability to hold and understand an overall picture of the application or product. Because of this, he or she can ensure that the application is built and used efficiently and consistently. Most projects larger than two or three programmers need at least one big-brained person, typically serving as lead architect or a similar role. Whether or not a project has one of these big-brained people, someone has to divide the project into independent pieces so that neither the development team nor the customer's team has to consist of all big-brained people.

Example

In the clothing repair framework, we don't want everyone to have to understand every aspect of the framework. For example, we'd like to allow the repair team to focus on the repair portion without having to worry about the details of any of the other pieces (such as selection and cleaning). We also don't want to make the framework user have to understand the entire framework to use any individual piece of it.

---

6. These are the people who can effectively put an entire large, complex system into their heads. For example, they can quickly tell you all the ramifications of a small change in one place on the entire system.

Problem

How do we divide the framework to reduce the need for big-brained people to build and consume the framework?

Approaches

The key idea here is to divide the problem into independent consumable pieces in such a way that you don't have to be a big-brained person to understand and use them. We've found a number of techniques that are effective for achieving this.

The first technique is to layer the framework. These layers are large chunks of the framework that you can decide to use or not. Each layer builds on the lower layer, and lower layers should not have any dependency on the upper layers. We found that, as shown in Figure 3.2, there are three core layers: a foundation layer (which includes the infrastructure), a cross-domain (or utility) layer, and a domain-specific layer. This doesn't mean you'll have exactly three layers; you should do what is appropriate for your particular situation.

The foundation layer contains the underlying utilities and functions that must be ubiquitous to the framework (for example, support for locale-sensitive descriptions, time stamps, or decimals). Often these are built by starting with an off-the-shelf infrastructure, such as Java or an Enterprise Java Beans application server, and, by adding specific usage patterns and utility classes, extending it to meet the needs common to your framework's domain.

In the cross-domain layer, things that are commonly needed for the framework's target domain are provided. In the IBM SanFrancisco project these were the

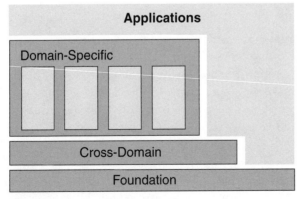

Figure 3.2   *Basic framework layers*

business objects and functions that any business application would need (for example, Company, which supports representing organizational structures, and Currency, which supports working with multiple currencies, including exchange rates).

The domain-specific layer contains things that are specific to particular domains. This layer usually is subdivided into individual, independent domains since you usually want to use all the support in a particular domain. In the IBM SanFrancisco project these were the business objects and functions that were specific to application domains (for example, specific domains like the General Ledger domain and the Warehouse domain). In that project these domain-specific subdivisions were independent of one another.

The three layers used in the IBM SanFrancisco project are shown in Figure 3.3. The foundation layer, which was based on Java, was simply called the Foundation. The cross-domain layer was called the Common Business Objects, and the domain-specific layer was called the Core Business Process (CBP). In particular the General Ledger (GL) and Warehouse Management (WM) CBPs are shown.

When working on the clothing framework, we find that a commercially available application server (WebSphere Advanced Server[7]) provides all the functions we need from a foundation layer, but we still need a common cross-domain layer. This common layer consists of the business objects common to each aspect of our clothing framework, such as the ClothingItem business

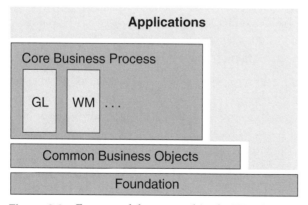

Figure 3.3 *Framework layers used in the IBM SanFrancisco project*

7. Information is available online at http://www.ibm.com/software/webservers/appserv/.

object. When we evaluate our planned framework at the domain-specific layer, we don't subdivide its contents since its pieces (selection, repair, and so on) are ones we would use together.

Once we have divided the framework into layers, we divide the layers into component categories. Usually the division into layers is done as part of the overall architecture definition and the division into categories is done during analysis. Since category definition is performed as part of analysis, it is discussed in the Eating the Elephant pattern (see Section 5.1).

This layering and subsequent categorization allow the framework developers and consumers to focus on particular aspects of the framework without having to understand the entire framework. Also, it makes it easier for framework consumers to decide which pieces of the framework they want to use, first deciding which layers to use and then which categories within those layers.

No matter which technique you decide to use, you have to be flexible—especially at the beginning. You won't get everything into the right layer the first time and, as you'll see in the Eating the Elephant pattern, you definitely won't get your categories exactly right. You should be cautious about moving things— you don't want to play Ping-Pong, but you shouldn't completely stifle change.

Another approach, which isn't mutually exclusive to layering, is to look at the coarse-grained components that will be built with the framework (see Appendix A). These coarse-grained components need to be independent of one another, so the developers need to make sure the framework's pieces can be effectively used without excessive coupling. To do this between all the pieces would make the framework unusable. If you are planning to support coarse-grained components, you need to partition the framework with this in mind. At this level partitioning is only logical, and when designing you will have to choose from a number of techniques for keeping independence.

You can use other alternative architectural approaches, and, as mentioned above, architectural approaches can be combined as appropriate. Whichever approach you decide to use, the key is to try to divide the framework into large chunks with well-defined dependencies such that the framework can be understood and consumed in stages, rather than all at once.

Solution

- Break the framework into large chunks in order to
  - Create well-defined dependencies.
  - Improve understandability.
  - Improve the ability of users to understand the framework.

- When dividing up the framework, keep in mind how the framework will be used.
- Consider layering the framework to make it easier to build and consume.
  - The foundation layer adds utility to the underlying technology.
  - The cross-domain layer provides items needed by everyone in the framework's target domain.
  - The domain-specific layer covers items specific to a domain and may be subdivided.
- Layers can be broken down into categories—see the Eating the Elephant pattern (Section 5.1).
- Don't be trapped by your layers (or other divisions). Especially in the beginning, they are guidelines. Things will move between the layers as development moves forward.
- If you're using the framework to build coarse-grained components, some partitioning may be necessary to allow independent usage.
- Other approaches and hybrid approaches are possible.

When to Use/Not Use

You don't want to kill a gnat with a 16-ton weight, and you don't want to take an extremely small framework and partition it. If the partitioning benefits the development and consumption of the framework, then use it. If it doesn't, don't. The key is to break up the framework into chunks that make sense for your framework from both understandability and usability perspectives.

This approach can be (and often is) used for any software development. Any large piece of software can benefit from being broken into consumable pieces.

Applicability

- Make sure the framework needs to be broken up before doing so.
- Partitioning applies to software development in general.

Known Uses

This technique has been used in the development of many hardware and software systems. During the development of the IBM SanFrancisco frameworks we felt that it was an important technique for making the framework not only more understandable but also more consumable. Since we divided the framework as shown in Figure 3.3, a framework user could decide at what layer to use the framework—only using the Foundation, using the Common Business Objects (and Foundation), or using all layers of the framework including one or more of the Core Business Processes.

Related Pattern

- Eating the Elephant (Section 5.1)—further subdivision occurs during analysis.

3.4 Consistency Is King

Also Known As

Maintain Consistency throughout the Framework

Intent

One of the best things you can do to improve the understandability and usability of your framework (or any other software) is to be consistent.

Context

You can go anywhere in the world and drive a car. There will be slight differences, such as which side the steering wheel is on, but every car will have a steering wheel. This consistency makes it possible to quickly overcome the slight differences and safely drive the car. Cruise control, which maintains a certain speed, is another matter entirely. Some cars have buttons on the wheel; some sticks you have to rotate; some levers you have to push. Does consistency really matter? For the big stuff like steering wheels it does, but for little things like cruise control it probably doesn't.

What would happen if we didn't have consistent steering wheels? If you walked out to your rental car and it had foot levers to steer and hand controls for brakes and speed, what would you do? I don't know how far you'd get, but it would certainly be an exciting trip. On the other hand, cruise control isn't critical. You can drive the car without it, but you can look up in the owner's manual how to engage cruise control if you really want to use it.

So what does this have to do with software? Most people have experience with some kind of look and feel; at least they've probably seen the standard Windows interface. These look-and-feel rules are all about consistency. For example, take the recurring problem of how to manage and manipulate windows. Now, just like you can drive any car, you can work with the windows in any program. Does this matter? Before consistent look-and-feel guidelines were established, it was confusing having to figure out how to do the same thing in each application. The keystroke that closed one application's windows caused other applications to minimize their windows!

Reusable software is in exactly the same situation. There are many places where the same problem is going to be solved. If all occurrences are solved consistently, it is infinitely easier for framework users to consume the framework. They are able to learn the pattern (or approach) the first time they encounter it and then leverage that knowledge the next time.

Example

Remember our example from the Alles in Ordnung pattern (see Section 3.1)? In that example, we designed and implemented two sections of our clothing framework using different approaches. When developing the clothing repair framework, we encapsulated the repair algorithm in a method. To customize the repair algorithm the framework user has to subclass the framework class and replace the method with one that implements the new algorithm. On the other hand, when we developed the selection algorithm we implemented it using the Strategy design pattern [Gamma 94]. The selection algorithm is pulled out into a separate strategy object that can be independently replaced. The user simply implements the strategy object's Java interface and replaces the default (simple) strategy shipped with the framework with the customized implementation.

Now get into the transformation booth and become the consumer of this framework. One of the first questions we'd probably ask is, "Why are these different?" Are there differences in requirements that led to the two solutions? When we go to look at the requirements, which may not be available, we might be able to figure out why, or we may not. If the reason they are different is because one developer knew about design patterns and the other didn't, we may never be able to figure it out. This won't bother some people, but it will drive others crazy.

While in this case there were probably nonfunctional requirements (the need for adaptations at runtime) that actually drove the decision, there will be cases where it isn't as clear. The designer may have gone beyond the requirements, allowing adaptation at runtime when it isn't needed. Or the designer may have multiple patterns to choose from that can fulfill the same requirements. There will even be cases where the decision was arbitrary (which, when possible, should also be made consistently).

These inconsistencies will especially bother the domain experts who are trying to map their requirements to your requirements. In many cases they are already struggling with the new technologies used by the framework, so you really don't want to put any more barriers in their way.

In addition, the development team didn't leverage what they learned solving the problem the first time when solving the problem again. In our example, the developer who discovered the design pattern and applied it had to determine whether the pattern really fulfilled the needs and probably addressed a number of issues applying the pattern. This knowledge would have accelerated the application of the pattern the second time.

Problem

Unnecessary inconsistency will confuse framework consumers. Knowledge obtained in one part of the framework cannot be leveraged. Everything has to be done from scratch.

Approaches

We've found that consistency has to be achieved iteratively in four phases: identification, specification, education, and enforcement. *Identification* is the process of finding opportunities for consistency. *Specification* is documenting when and how to be consistent. *Education* is ensuring that everyone knows what has been identified and specified. *Enforcement* is making sure that when there is a consistent way to do it, it is done that way.

Identification

Identifying opportunities for consistency can be as simple as just being alert and waiting for them to come to you or it can be a rigorous rooting out of every possible iota of consistency. Reality is usually between these two extremes.

Just being alert to the existence of consistency will help you find it. You'll realize you've heard a question before or that you are coming up with a similar solution to a new problem. In fact, you probably are doing this already. Everyone, at some time or another, has realized that they already have (or could get) something that solved a similar problem to the one they're trying to solve. This approach of copying (or acquiring) as a reuse methodology can create consistency simply because, to some extent, the structure of the original is retained.

A more rigorous approach to identifying consistency opportunities usually involves some level of explicit process. The most likely points where consistency should be identified is during knowledge transfer points (as discussed in the Innocent Questions pattern, Section 3.2) within the development process. At these points a critical mass of project members come together to exchange information. During that process, the participants should be looking not only to give out or gain information but also to discover similarities between what is being discussed and other areas of the project.

Specification

Specifying consistency can be a challenge—how far should you go to define rules for development? Consistency can be defined both "in the large" and "in the small." What do we mean by this? Consistency "in the large" deals with core development principles: what level of detail should be specified in requirements documents, how designs are evaluated, what type of information should be documented in source code interfaces, and so on. Consistency "in the small" addresses the details of development: how requirements documents should be formatted, how design models should be represented, how attributes and parameters should be formatted, and so on. We believe that specifying consistency "in the large" is in general more important than consistency "in the small," although many elements of consistency "in the small" lead to a more usable and maintainable framework.

The core principle involved in specifying consistency is to use and develop standards, both those that are widely accepted throughout the software industry (such as the Unified Modeling Language and Javadoc), as well as those defined within your development group (such as specifying the core set of design patterns that should be followed as framework components are developed). As we discuss in the Consistency Czar pattern (see Section 8.3), we believe that these standards should grow naturally with a project. Don't try to define a full-fledged set of standards on the first day of your development project—you are sure to overspecify in some areas and completely miss other areas that you will eventually recognize as crucial to your project's success. Instead, start with a set of basic consistency principles and build on that set over time. If you have previous experience in developing a similar project or projects in the past, spend some time up front reviewing the standards from those projects and deciding which should be applied to your current project. This can give you a big jump start in making your development team more effective from day one.

We believe that consistency "in the large" is most effectively defined in the form of patterns. Patterns can provide useful abstractions at all stages of development. While patterns in software development are most often considered in the design phase, they are just as applicable in the analysis and requirements phases of development. *Analysis Patterns* [Fowler 97] and *Writing Effective Use Cases* [Cockburn 00] are prime examples of formal and informal patterns defined at the analysis and requirements levels of development, respectively.

Likewise, consistency "in the small" can often be defined as idioms—style examples that can show developers how to write particular use cases, present analysis classes within a class diagram, create logging entries in source code, and so on.

If your project is large enough, you might consider dealing with consistency "in the small" by developing or customizing tools and templates. One good example is a code-generation tool that takes much of the tedium out of writing the many lines of boilerplate code required for most classes. Code-generation tools also make it much easier to make changes in the programming model. The generated code can either be regenerated or programmatically changed. Templates, such as one that lays out how use cases should be written, can also serve this purpose, acting as a starting point with examples for the team to follow.

Education

As you specify consistency rules, you of course need to educate your team on those rules. In this stage, you are taking advantage of the consistency rules and guidelines you have documented in the prior specification stage. You will find that project size, development culture, and level of developer experience will all affect the style in which you provide consistency education. It's been our experience that informal approaches to education are most effective once a consistency foundation has been established more formally (for example, through tutorials and classes). Not surprisingly, both forms of education are more effective when the concepts being taught can be shown through concrete examples and then immediately applied. For example, we've found that the best way to teach patterns (or any abstract concept) is to first show a number of examples and then show how those examples can be abstracted into a broadly applicable pattern.

Enforcement

Finally, your consistency rules need to be enforced throughout the development life cycle. The Consistency Czar pattern (see Section 8.3) focuses on this task and its interplay with the other phases of consistency management discussed above. We won't go into the details here, but we do want to point out that those responsible for enforcing consistency within a development project must not only identify and correct points of inconsistency but also recognize where existing consistency rules aren't sufficient, either adapting those rules (and determining if and when to apply those modified rules throughout already developed portions of the project) or perhaps allowing the inconsistency to remain because of extenuating circumstances. In effect, the enforcement stage involves all the other stages in an iterative cycle, just as a good software development process incorporates iteration throughout the software development life cycle.

Solution

- Be aware that consistency exists. Search for opportunities to define and apply consistency guidelines.
- Use, define, and document standards.
  - Take advantage of existing industry standards when applicable.
  - Define appropriate standards for all deliverables.
  - Tools and templates are useful for simplifying the implementation of standards. Consider in particular code-generation tools to minimize the need to write boilerplate code.
  - Use patterns and idioms to document abstractions that should be broadly applied throughout the framework.
- Educate team members through both formal (tutorials and classes) and informal (one-on-one mentoring) means.
- Assign a Consistency Czar (see Section 8.3).
- Iterate as needed to update and maintain consistency standards.

When to Use/Not Use

Some level of consistency is important for any software development project. The larger the scale of the project and the more the output of your project is likely to be used by others, the more consistency is required. Don't underestimate the potential amount of reuse for your project—it's very difficult to put consistency back into a project not developed with consistency in mind, and if what you thought would be an isolated piece of software becomes heavily used by others, you (or whoever is maintaining that software) will wish that consistency rules had been applied more rigorously during project development. On the flip side, however, don't spend your energy defining and enforcing consistency rules that don't provide much value to the developers and users of the software.

Applicability

- Take into account the size of your project.
- Assume your code will be reused more than you expect.
- Focus your limited energy on the consistency issues that give the most benefit.

Known Uses

Most software projects and development organizations define some form of consistency rules. Often (although not exclusively) these rules are concentrated at the latter stages of the development cycle. In the IBM SanFrancisco project, as is appropriate for large-scale framework development, we defined consistency rules at all stages of software development. Many of our design rules have been codified into design patterns and published in *SanFrancisco Design Patterns: Blueprints for Business Software* [Carey 00].

Related Patterns

- Alles in Ordnung (Section 3.1)—each phase of consistency needs to be part of your process.
- Consistency Czar (Section 8.3)—specific strategies help manage the enforcement phase of consistency.

3.5 Iterate, Iterate, Iterate

Also Known As

Three Iterations to Validate

Intent

As with any object-oriented software development, iteration is an integral aspect of framework development. For a framework, the key iterations involve refining it to its target domain. There are things you can do to reduce the number of iterations and maximize the effectiveness of each iteration.

Context

Picture yourself as a chef trying to create the core of a new recipe. You need this core recipe to be something you can use as the basis for creating dishes for entering and winning contests, for feeding your family, and for use in your restaurant. You take these requirements and your domain knowledge and create a first attempt at the recipe. Now you can start creating dishes with it. First you use it to feed your family. You find out that it is missing a key spice that makes the recipe much better for feeding the family and better in general. So, you update the recipe and then try using it in your restaurant. You discover that cooking the increased quantity makes processing of one of the ingredients impractical. This problem with quantity drives you to figure out a less labor-intensive ingredient as a substitution. Why not change the recipe to the new ingredient? The recipe is used to feed the family and the customers in the restaurant; you can't change the recipe for the restaurant and forget about the family. The alternative ingredient could be used when making the recipe for the family, but the food tastes much better with the original ingredient. Thus you allow a substitution (extension point) instead of simply replacing the item in the recipe. After this refinement, you use the recipe to make a dish for a contest, but you find that it requires more work than you can complete in the allotted hour. Again, you need to refine it—keeping in mind the other uses. When finished you have a core recipe that you can use as the basis of a dish for any of these circumstances.

If you read about frameworks, you rapidly discover that this kind of iteration is at the heart of framework development. Ralph Johnson says that three different uses of a framework are necessary to refine it to the point where it is stable enough to be applied to most problems in its target domain [Johnson 02]. These different uses cause refinement across all aspects of framework development from requirements down to code. However, most projects don't have the luxury (or investor money) to find three uses for a framework before shipping it as a product. This means that somehow the number of uses (and iterations) must be minimized and, at the same time, each use must achieve maximum effectiveness. The best way to do this is to find ways to move the iteration that would have been caused by the three uses into the development of the framework. Even then, the number and amount of development iteration needs to be minimized. The idealistic (and completely unrealistic) goal is to complete a framework without having any explicit uses and without any iteration.

Example

In the clothing example, when the selection portion of the framework was developed, it was first targeted at casual wear only. When work began on requirements gathering, it was discovered or perhaps remembered (possibly from applying the Innocent Questions pattern, Section 3.2) that the framework has to also support formal wear. This requirement then had to be rolled back into the completed requirements, thus causing iteration. As development continued into the design phase, discussion on how to support some variability (possibly from applying the Tor's Second Cousin pattern, Section 4.2) led to the realization that the framework also has to support clown wear. This new requirement thus had to be rolled back into the requirements and then brought forward into the analysis and design phases. This process continued at every level of development and could even occur after customers use the first release of the product.

Problem

Refinement iterations are expensive and time consuming, but their results are crucial to making a successful framework. How can we get the same results with fewer but more intense iterations?

Approaches

None of the approaches described in this chapter will totally remove iteration from the development process since iteration is in effect a rework scheduling strategy that is crucial to effective software development [Cockburn 98]. Instead, if applied effectively, these approaches will reduce the scope of the iterations. In other words, a change in requirements during a requirements phase is much less painful than a change in requirements after customers report problems in the first release of the product. Not surprisingly, since in one sense iteration is caused by errors, this parallels error identification in software development. Sooner is cheaper and later is expensive—and potentially embarrassing. That isn't to say that all iterations are caused by mistakes. As with errors, there is usually a misunderstanding at the crux of iteration. The first and foremost thing that can be done to reduce the scope of iteration is to reduce misunderstandings and identify them as soon as possible.[8] Many of the techniques described in other sections address this problem. For example, having separate domain and technical experts is a situation ripe for misunderstandings. Being aware of this potential and turning it around, for example,

---

8. If when applying the Alles in Ordnung pattern (see Section 3.1) you decided to use the Extreme Programming process, you would also be addressing this by focusing on a piecewise understanding and building the product via iteration. In this case iteration is not being caused by errors. Examples of errors that could lead to further iteration include the discovery of additional bugs and the discovery of additional user stories for items believed to be completed.

by using the Innocent Questions pattern (see Section 3.2), can reduce the misunderstandings.

Another place ripe for misunderstandings is the requirements section. Coming from the viewpoint of software development, most developers have a desire to create bulletproof requirements that hopefully lead to bulletproof code, but we cannot do this in framework development (see the Pass the Buck pattern, Section 6.1). And, as described in the What, Not How pattern (see Section 4.3), it is easy to fall into the trap of using a prior implementation as the requirements. Avoiding or at least reducing these misunderstandings is a crucial part of reducing the scope of iterations. The better the requirements are, the less likely the need to iterate back and modify them—or at least the smaller the change when we do.

While this is a good starting point, another crucial aspect is domain expertise. If the framework is intended to be used in a specific area, such as clown wear, and you don't have an expert in clown wear, how are you going to know if the framework you're building can really be used by clowns? Mistakes will be made when determining and evaluating the clown wear requirements. This is a tradeoff. You must have some domain experts, but the likelihood that you will be able to find and afford one for each target area of the framework may be small. There are a few individuals out there, some of whom we've had the pleasure of working with, who know many aspects of a domain intimately. These individuals are rare, and we recommend keeping them happy and on your team. When you can't find these individuals, you have to hire a number of domain experts, each with different areas of focus. Hire them in the order of importance to the framework of their particular expertise. In our clothing example, we would hire a casual clothing selection expert first since we believe that is the biggest market for the framework. Next we'd hire a formal clothing selection expert and, only after filling those two positions, a clothing expert for clowns.

There is also a social aspect of domain teams (see the There Is No "I" in Team pattern, Section 8.1). We recommend that you hire at least two domain experts, since they provide a check and balance for one another. Unfortunately, two experts can sometimes reach an impasse on any particular topic, so it's often useful to have a third domain expert—who might also be the chief domain expert (see below), system architect, or business lead on the project—to break the ties that will naturally occur. However, you should be cautious about putting more than three domain experts on the same team.

If you can't get an expert to cover each targeted area, are you out of luck? Not necessarily; there are a number of approaches you can use in this case. One technique we have used successfully is to identify one chief domain expert. This person, in our case, was the individual with the broadest knowledge. He was not on a development team, but he reviewed what each team was doing and acted as an arbitrator in disputes. This allowed us to leverage this individual's broad knowledge and gave us someone whom the other domain experts accepted as an arbitrator. Having someone look at everything has tremendous benefits. He or she can recognize similarities (see the Consistency Czar pattern, Section 8.3) and get the teams to collaborate—ensuring knowledge is not stuck in one particular team.

Another approach we have successfully used is to form an advisory council. In the case of the IBM SanFrancisco project, this council consisted of domain experts from companies that were interested in using the framework. Periodically the requirements, analysis models, and designs were presented to this council for review. In this way we were able to gain access to key domain experts in our expected customer set and get their candid feedback. This feedback was invaluable for validating both that we hadn't missed areas we should be supporting and that we were putting in the correct amount of variability support. How often you bring the information to the advisory council is again a tradeoff. Most companies will give up only a limited amount of their domain experts' time, and presenting information and harvesting feedback is a time-consuming process. However, some will give you all the time you want. Assuming you can work through any legal problems, these are cases where you may want to look at making such experts part of your development team.

In addition to domain expertise, you'll need technical expertise. We haven't found any magical solution to this need. For an object-oriented framework, you need a core group of object-oriented experts. The exact size of the group depends on the size of your development effort. This core team must be able to work well with the domain experts since conflict will lead to misunderstandings and mistakes—and thus iteration. Having a formal development process with clear deliverables and owners (see the Alles in Ordnung pattern, Section 3.1) can help. This keeps people focused on their roles and responsibilities and helps to ensure that things don't fall through the cracks.

Another way to reduce the scope of iteration is to create a separate (independent) testing team that builds simple applications from the framework. This team, by approaching the framework from a different perspective (trying to use it rather than develop it), ends up asking questions that help clarify and refine all aspects of the framework. This team can begin as soon as the requirements are considered done, but even if they can't start right away, any time they can begin will be beneficial. For example, in the clothing selection framework the "abstracted" requirements didn't take into account how a user interface built on an application based on the framework would retrieve information. Obtaining such feedback on this first portion of the framework allows us to quickly fix the problem and then ensure it is taken into account during development of the rest of the framework. Beta testers—customers who are willing to take early versions of the framework and try to use them— form another independent team that can help in this regard.

Solution

- Refinement iteration is a fact of life—try to reduce the scope by reducing misunderstandings and miscommunications:
  - Within the domain expert team
  - Between the domain experts and technical experts
  - Between the development team and the customers
- Domain expertise is crucial.
  - Try to get domain experts for all domain areas targeted by the framework.
  - Identify a chief domain expert to review all work and act as the arbitrator.
  - Form an advisory council of customers to review the framework.
- Technical expertise is crucial.
  - Establish a core group of technical experts. Not all technical experts will thrive in this environment.
  - Use a formal development process to reduce misunderstandings.
- Customer perspective is important.
  - Advisory council gives early feedback.
  - Test team gives early usage feedback.
  - Beta testers (customers) give early customer usage feedback.

When to Use/Not Use

These approaches can be used whenever you are developing reusable software. However, software being developed for a particular use shouldn't follow these approaches. In that case, specific use cases can be provided for the specific problem to be solved. Iteration will still occur because of misunderstandings, but these can be addressed in a more traditional manner.

Applicability

- Use these approaches whenever you're developing reusable software.

Known Uses

We have used these approaches (individually and in groups) on many of the development projects we've worked on, including the IBM SanFrancisco project.

Related Patterns

- Alles in Ordnung (Section 3.1)—following a development process can help reduce misunderstandings by ensuring that there are clear deliverables and owners.
- Innocent Questions (Section 3.2)—encouraging communication between the two groups helps reduce misunderstandings.
- Tor's Second Cousin (Section 4.2)—decide how much variability to support and make sure the range of variability is understood.
- What, Not How (Section 4.3)—reduce misunderstandings by ensuring you have good requirements.
- Pass the Buck (Section 6.1)—recognize when technical team members may cause problems by trying to create bulletproof code.
- There Is No "I" in Team (Section 8.1)—recognize that social aspects can cause misunderstandings.
- Consistency Czar (Section 8.3)—a domain lead can help ensure consistency.

3.6 Exposing It All

Also Known As

A Framework's Customer Is Its Partner

Intent

The framework user is a partner with the framework development team. The framework has to expose enough to make the user successful without making everything part of the product.

Context

The salesperson says this magic elixir will solve all your problems—hair loss, weight loss, and whatever else ails you. Why don't you believe? Even if somehow the salesperson convinces you to plunk down your money, will you actually drink the potion when you get home? By then you may realize you really don't know what it is or how to find out. You might look for the mandatory ingredient label, but you'll find it just says "good stuff and secret ingredients." Are you like Alice? Will you drink it and find yourself in Wonderland? Or do you throw it out and have a soda instead? Put yourself into the framework user's shoes. Isn't it about the same? A salesperson has told you how wonderful the framework is, you've bought it and brought it home. Now you really want to do something with it—can you?

A framework is not like other software products for which there is a user interface or Application Programming Interface (API) hiding the consumer from the actual implementation details. For example, I really don't need to know the internals of a class library to use it. I'm happy if the documentation says it follows the Institute of Electrical and Electronics Engineers (IEEE) standard when it calculates cosine for me. I really don't care how it works. On the other hand, is it sufficient for a framework to document its support just in terms of standards? Actually, if it can do that, it probably isn't a framework—or at least it's a case where a framework isn't needed. Frameworks are built to support customization and extensibility—providing a core architecture, design, and implementation that can be customized to your particular needs. If all the needs are the same, they could be provided simply by a class library.

If I can't just document the APIs of the framework classes, what do I have to document as part of the product? How do I know what is enough and what is too much?

Example

In the clothing selection aspect of our case study, for example, we could simply document that there is a selectClothing method that selects the clothing. Sadly, we've seen this kind of documentation, and we're sure you have too. So now you know what it does. How does it work? How do you customize it to select clothing in a way that conforms to your requirements? In fact, how do you even determine whether it can fulfill your requirements? You need to know what the architecture and design are so that you can figure this out. You also need to know of any patterns that are used—and how they are used in this situation. If the framework doesn't include this information, you either won't be able to use it to build your clothing application or you'll have a very difficult time (and you'll probably eventually walk away from the framework and build a new one yourself—the time-tested approach to which every software developer seems to naturally gravitate).

Problem

A framework requires exposure of more of its details than other types of software do. How do you determine what to expose and what to leave hidden?

Approaches

We've found that for frameworks to succeed you have to get into the mindset that you are a partner with the framework users. Your success depends on their success. This quickly leads you to realize that you have to provide almost everything. We've found that the crucial elements of framework documentation are the requirements, use cases, analysis models, design models, patterns, programming model, and Javadoc or equivalent documentation that specifies the behavior of individual methods of your framework. In fact, we've found we even need to supplement these with documents that are not normal development artifacts, such as examples, user guides, and books. On the other hand, the things we think you have a choice about exposing are the source code (at least for the immutable portions of the framework) and the test cases.

One of framework users' key goals is to map to the framework as early as possible in the development cycle. This is also known as gap analysis—the objective here is to discover where the framework fully or partially meets their needs by comparing their requirements against the requirements the framework supports. The sooner users can map to the framework, the greater the reuse (and thus the greater the jump start) they can obtain. Also, at these high levels the details don't get in the way of the comparison. For example, a user may need a process for picking product in a warehouse, but he or she doesn't need to know all the details of how the picking is done—at this point. If the requirements, use cases, and analysis models are not provided, how can the user do this mapping? Not many people are going to try to work these out from the framework's interface documentation. In fact, if they have to, wouldn't it be easier just to write it themselves?

Just as the domain experts need the high-level artifacts to map to the framework as early as possible, the developers need the design models, programming model and patterns documentation to complete their mapping process against the framework. These allow them to determine what they need to do to fulfill their application's requirements and map from their design to the framework (see the Map Early, Map Often pattern, Section 9.2). The programming model and patterns documentation may have to be cleaned up for this delivery. What was sufficient internally may not be good enough to ship as part of a product. Also, developing a framework is different from developing an application on a framework, so this has to be reflected in these documents. For example, the goal of a framework is to be flexible so it can be used for many possible applications. This means that some things are done to ensure this flexibility. Applications developers, who know exactly what flexibility they need and where and when they need it, can decide when to use simpler approaches rather than the more flexible approaches used in frameworks. Since these documents were developed for and during framework development, they will not naturally contain this type of discussion. The delivery of Javadoc is just like any other software—it documents the actual classes and APIs developers use to implement their applications.

Throughout the various levels of framework documentation, you should also consider providing additional documentation above and beyond the artifacts directly related to the framework. The framework is an abstract core solution for many applications. Most people don't easily grasp abstract things. Instead they see a number of concrete examples and then can be led to the abstraction. This normal way of understanding abstractions means that simply giving the domain expert the framework artifacts may not be enough (see the Give 'Em What They Want pattern, Section 7.2). An example is how to deal with names of domain concepts that have been abstracted. It is difficult to explain what a dissection is to a financial person who has a different term for it. However, showing how a dissection would be used to solve the problem allows an accountant familiar with U.S. accounting to quickly recognize it as a journal entry. This is especially true when powerful new ways of solving a problem have been discovered and provided with the framework. Starting where the normal users are (in other words, using terms and concepts with which they are familiar and comfortable) and moving them to your solution is the only way to successfully help them understand and then use the framework.

You can use numerous approaches to give customers this contextual documentation. One valuable approach is to offer user guides that provide domain-level descriptions of the framework, some starting from domain-specific examples. For example, the IBM SanFrancisco frameworks provided a user guide for the general ledger that talked about the core abstractions it provided, and it had another companion guide that talked about a U.S. general ledger and how this would be implemented using the IBM SanFrancisco frameworks.

Another approach is to provide sample applications. These are simple, complete applications that allow the user to see how the framework is used. As the word *sample* implies, the source code for these examples is provided.

Sometimes a complete sample application won't be required; instead, you can simply provide additional sample analysis and design models that show how the framework could be used to support a particular application. Note that providing these solutions can be expensive and, since they are targeted at domain experts, should be done with lots of input from your domain experts.

All of the documentation elements discussed above must be shipped with the framework. Beyond these elements, there are a couple of additional artifacts that, if you're like us, will spark heated debates. One such artifact is the framework's source code—should this code be provided as documentation? This provides the ultimate documentation, since it exposes exactly what is done. Unfortunately, it also removes any possible hiding place. Why would you even consider this? The source code provides a starting point for extending the framework. An existing framework class can be copied, modified, and then used to replace the framework class or serve as a new class. Without the source code, either the existing implementation would need to be extended or all of the code rewritten from scratch. Another point of contention is the test cases used for framework development. These can be useful to customers as an installation validation test and as a starting point for their own testing. However, as described in the Consistency Czar pattern (see Section 8.3), this may be a place where you want to give developers freedom. If so, it's not a good idea to deliver test cases to customers.

In each of the above artifacts there are three things you must consider when deciding what, if anything, you'll deliver with the framework.

1. *Intellectual property* becomes a concern because of how much information is being exposed. Normally you have just the API to worry about, but if you include all these artifacts with your framework, you have to worry about someone using your domain analysis and design models for another project.

2. *Service and support* becomes an issue because of the increase in product artifacts. You can solve this problem by delivering some items "as is." For example, the sample applications could be delivered this way.

3. *Cost* has a large impact on the artifacts delivered with the framework. You have to decide who is going to create the artifacts and to what level of detail they will be created (see the Souvenirs pattern, Section 7.1). Some are already part of your normal development process, but how much do you want to spend to clean them up for delivery? Do you want to hire contractors to do the work? How polished do you want to make them? For example, it would be ideal if the artifacts linked back and forth between one another, so a user could start anywhere and easily navigate to other related artifacts.

The most important thing you can do is break out of the "bulletproof vest" mentality that says you have protection from your users seeing anything more than the software's APIs. To succeed, the framework customers have to be treated like partners.

Solution

- Realize that the framework customer is your partner. As a partner, your customer will need to see and use more than just the software's APIs.
- There are several artifacts you should deliver.
  - Development artifacts: requirements, use cases, analysis models, design models
  - Contextual documents: user guide (the domain perspective and sample mappings), sample applications (simple applications to demonstrate use), programming model and patterns documentation (updated with framework user's perspective)
- There are some artifacts you should consider delivering.
  - Source code
  - Test cases
- Think about the following issues as you decide which artifacts to include.
  - Intellectual property—do you want to try to protect it?
  - Service and support—do you want to deliver some items "as is"?
  - Cost—how much are you willing to spend?

When to Use/Not Use

You must keep in mind who will be using the framework. If the team members who developed the framework will be the only users of the framework, this is not an issue. They already have access to all of the information and have an understanding of what the framework can and can't do. However, the longevity of the framework needs to be considered. If the framework will be used for a long time, these artifacts can be used to capture knowledge that may otherwise be lost as team members move to other projects.

These artifacts become more important as the size and scope of the framework increase. A product with multiple interacting frameworks that address a number of domains needs extensive documentation much more than a simple framework with three classes.

If your framework has been divided into pieces, as described in the Divide and Conquer pattern (see Section 3.3), you may have to make different decisions for each piece. A layer that provides the technical underpinnings, such as the foundation layer described in the Divide and Conquer pattern, does not need to deliver the same artifacts as a layer that provides customizable business processes.

Applicability

- The audience of the framework will dictate which artifacts you create and expose. Frameworks for internal consumption by the team that developed it can get away with much less.
- The importance of exposure increases with the size and complexity of the framework.
- Different framework pieces may have different levels of exposure.

Known Uses

For the IBM SanFrancisco project we provided the following artifacts as part of the product.

- **Requirements**—a high-level description of what the framework is intended to do.
- **Use cases**—high-level descriptions of interactions with the framework. Although for other types of software development these start from the application user, for a framework, since there isn't a specific application, they often start from the first use of what is provided by the framework.
- **Scenarios**—more detailed use cases that describe how the analysis objects work together to fulfill the requirements.
- **Analysis models**—high-level, domain-recognizable models of the objects and responsibilities of the framework solution.
- **Design models**—detailed models of the objects and responsibilities of the classes that are used to implement the analysis diagrams.
- **Interaction diagrams**—diagrams that show the interactions of the design-level objects. This is usually in support of a particular method call.
- **Javadoc**—description of the methods and their parameters for all of the APIs.
- **Source code**—coding for the business components but not the foundation layer (infrastructure code)—see the Divide and Conquer pattern (Section 3.3) for a discussion of the different layers.

- **Extension guide**—a how-to guide for customizing the framework's extension points.

- **Functional overview**—a description of the overall functions provided by the framework.

- **Glossary**—a list of terms with definitions.

- **User guides**—domain-centric descriptions of the functions provided by the framework. These approach the framework from a domain perspective and are where we expect domain experts to gain an understanding of the framework so they can determine how they can use it to build their applications.

- **Persistent object planning guide**—document that provides information about persisting the frameworks classes and their extensions.

- **Samples**—samples of how to use the framework.

Related Patterns

- Divide and Conquer (Section 3.3)—what you expose may change for different pieces of the framework.

- Souvenirs (Section 7.1)—how much money and time you are willing to spend to clean up artifacts and notes to make them part of the product helps determine what to include.

- Give 'Em What They Want (Section 7.2)—what you expose needs to be tailored to the audience you are trying to address.

- Consistency Czar (Section 8.3)—framework artifacts delivered to the customer need to maintain consistency, but you can give your team some freedom in areas not delivered to the customer.

- Map Early, Map Often (Section 9.2)—exposure is needed to help framework users map to the framework as early as possible.

Chapter
4

Requirements

Identifying and capturing requirements is the key to building a successful framework. A good start with requirements helps ensure that the framework is well focused and well founded. Sound requirements also ensure that the domain experts who will use the framework can understand it. The patterns that will help you when gathering requirements are

- It Depends (Section 4.1)—identifying the need for variability in the requirements
- Tor's Second Cousin (Section 4.2)—handling extreme requirements
- What, Not How (Section 4.3)—making sure that requirements as stated are truly requirements and not implementations
- The Stupid Test (Section 4.4)—deciding which requirements to include and which to omit

These patterns are described below.

4.1 It Depends

Also Known As

Identifying Customization

Intent

To find potential extension points (points of flexibility built into the framework) that have been missed, leverage your ignorance of the domain by asking leading questions and by listening to domain expert discussions and arguments.

Context

Back in the early days of automobiles, Henry Ford was famous for implementing modern production techniques, thereby making automobiles affordable to a much wider range of the public than was previously possible. One of the ways he did this was by limiting options such as color; in fact, he was quoted (perhaps apocryphally) as saying, "The customer can have any color Model T he wants so long as it's black."[1] While this was acceptable for some time, eventually his competitors started to produce autos in various colors. Ford was forced to respond, allowing customers to specify their color choices as a way to customize their automobiles. This trend continued in U.S. auto production to the point where customers could specify almost any combination of features they wanted. While this met the desires of a few customers, the vast majority weren't interested in this level of customization, and it also had the unfortunate side effect of increasing production costs. Most automobile manufacturers today take a middle-ground approach, providing a small number of options packages from which customers can choose when ordering automobiles. This gives their customers the customization flexibility they desire while allowing automakers to maintain better control over production processes.

How do we know if we have the right extension points in the framework? We start from the customization described in the requirements, but how do we know that those requirements are sufficiently flexible? How do we know that all of the potential extension points have been identified? Domain experts are only human, after all. They won't think of everything up front, so as with most development processes, the identification of extension points is an iterative

---

1. As quoted on http://www.modelt.org/tquotes.html.

process. We need to help drive these iterations so as to minimize their number and to speed up the development process. How can we do this? By leveraging our ignorance! Yes, our ignorance. (See the Innocent Questions pattern, Section 3.2.) With our limited knowledge of the domain we can ask questions that other domain people wouldn't ask. We are impartial observers who can swallow our pride and ask the stupid questions.

Often domain experts get tied up with the specifics of their examples or overestimate the need for supporting a particular nuance. They may argue that there is "only one way to do it and no other." Sometimes they are right, and sometimes they are wrong. Often teams of domain experts become embroiled in arguments, with some individuals thinking that other domain experts are trying to remove or downplay what they believe are key requirements. Such arguments can sometimes result from people being unwilling to admit (or seeming to admit) they are wrong. These domain experts are not moving beyond their own perspectives to see that this may be a place where both requirements are valid and both need to be supported. Other times these oversights are completely innocent—the experts just didn't consider customization or thought they didn't need to consider it because they felt it was implied in the requirements they had already written.

Example

In our clothing case study we listed the requirement of being able to select an item of clothing based on its appropriateness with other clothing. How do we determine appropriateness? How complex can appropriateness get? Imagine that two of our domain people are having a heated argument about the requirement for the environment to be part of the selection. One domain expert believes that appropriateness considerations should be limited to just situations like parties[2] and countries,[3] whereas the other thinks strongly it should include things like the weather and whether the wearer is going to be in a radioactive environment.

---

2. For example, birthday parties, garden parties with the queen, and so on. What is appropriate for a birthday party involving games such as bobbing for apples won't be appropriate when meeting with the queen at a garden party.

3. Different countries (and regions) have explicit and implied standards of what should be worn. For example, a bikini explicitly wouldn't be appropriate in Saudi Arabia. For implicit standards, just walk around and see what people are wearing. If everyone is wearing dark clothing, a fluorescent green coat might not be appropriate.

Problem

Because they are so familiar with the problem domain, it can often be hard for domain experts working on the requirements to recognize extension points; instead, they often see these aspects of the domain as implicitly documented or they become focused on specific approaches to the exclusion of others.

Approaches

As we look at questions of determining appropriateness, we need to realize that we don't know the answers. When we aren't domain experts in a particular area, we should never guess at the answer, since this can (and will) be disastrous. Instead, we should ask the domain expert our questions and listen to the answers. Sometimes we might need to ask our questions more than once, and sometimes we may need to take a break and come back to ask them another day. No matter what, we push to get the answer we need, but we don't push too much.

As we ask our questions, we need to listen very carefully for key phrases. Our favorite key phrase is "It depends." This is a clear signal that an extension point is probably needed. If our domain expert says, "It depends," we become like a hound dog on a scent, trying to determine what kind of extension point it is (and applying the rules in the other chapters).

Another key phrase sometimes uttered by a domain expert is "It always works that way." As unlikely as it may seem, this does happen. Normally this sort of response occurs when the technical team brings up some "cool" technical solution that would allow the framework to do something that an application in the domain would never consider doing. For example, putting in a rules engine to capture the nuances of clothing appropriateness may seem like a cool technical solution, but since all of the applications in our domain have a simple view of appropriateness, it is something we just wouldn't do. In general, increased flexibility comes at the expense of added complexity. Sometimes this added complexity is appropriate, but care should be taken to avoid "creeping elegance": feature-rich software that is next to impossible to comprehend or use. Excessive application of design patterns can often result in creeping elegance. When software developers first discover and understand the power of design patterns, they often apply patterns everywhere—even where they are inappropriate. We discuss this topic further in Missed It by That Much (see Section 6.2).

What about the radioactive environment argument from our example? This is another opportunity to ask if there is an extension point. Often domain experts are so focused on making the point that their way is the only way that they don't consider the fact that the other domain person may be right. Yes, we are dealing with humans! Sometimes asking, innocently of course, whether this might be an extension point gets the domain experts to step back and see that this is the case. At other times, they'll look at you like you're insane and continue their argument.

Solution

- Ask questions of the domain experts and listen to their answers.
  - Leverage your ignorance of the domain—ask leading questions to clarify customization needs.
  - Listen to how domain people respond to questions. Listen for key phrases (for example, "It depends") that indicate the need for customization.
  - Listen to domain experts arguing. Often the points of contention are extension points.

When to Use/Not Use

When you got your first hammer, the whole world appeared as nails that needed hammering. It is too easy to use this pattern to make everything an extension point. Don't assume that because you got an "It depends" answer that you have to have an extension point. You may have to ask other questions, related to other patterns, to determine whether this is truly an extension point and, if it is, whether it should be incorporated into the framework (see the Tor's Second Cousin pattern, Section 4.2).

Care must be taken when asking questions—they can affect domain experts in a manner much like the way physical elements are affected when observed (that is, the Heisenberg uncertainty principle).[4] If you don't ask the question carefully, you may influence the answer. Remember that you aren't the domain expert, and keep an eye out for them giving in too easily. You may have to repeatedly remind them how stupid you are (with respect to the domain) so that they are willing to push back and not accept what you say as "cast in concrete." For example, on the topic of clothing appropriateness, if you ask, "It would be easier if we kept appropriateness simple; should it really be that complex?" you've broken the uncertainty principle! The give-and-take to do this effectively grows over time, and as you and the domain experts become comfortable in your roles this becomes less and less of an issue.

---

4. The Heisenberg uncertainty principle states, "The more precisely the position is determined, the less precisely the momentum is known."

You have to listen carefully for hints. Each domain expert has favorite phrases that are equivalent to "It depends"; listen for and learn these. In addition, you need to spend enough time discussing a topic to sufficiently explore it. Don't try to deal with everything during one session. Coming back to a topic after an initial discussion often lets the subconscious mind mull over the topic, resulting in new insights. Sometimes these insights will be immediately apparent; other times you will have to ask multiple questions multiple times to pull out the truly valuable extension points.

Applicability

- Use this pattern to help identify potential extension points.
- Use the Tor's Second Cousin pattern (see Section 4.2) to refine these potential extension points, narrowing them to the ones that should be provided with the framework.
- Don't become overzealous—otherwise everything becomes an extension point.
- Don't forget that sometimes there won't be an extension point.
- When talking with domain experts, don't influence the answers by how you ask the questions.
- Listen carefully.
- Don't rush resolution; sometimes having time to think works wonders.

Known Uses

We relied heavily on this technique when developing the IBM SanFrancisco frameworks. For example, when we were creating the domain validation support, our entire domain team seemed to break into two camps. One camp believed that the only way to handle domain validation was to fail (throw the exception) on the first validation failure encountered. The other camp felt that as many validation failures as possible should be collected together before the failure (exception). This became a very heated discussion. Both solutions were right and equally valid. By simply asking, "Is this an extension point?" the discussion suddenly moved to what kind of customization was needed and how it could be provided, instead of how stupid the other domain experts were for thinking anyone would ever do it their way. We ended up providing a way to allow the framework user to control bundling of validation failures.

We also applied this technique when discussing how to calculate currency exchange rates. At first glance it appears that the only way to look up exchange rates is to find an exact match. That is, when asking for the exchange rate between U.S. dollars and Australian dollars, we must find an entry for the requested date between those currencies. When we asked the domain person whether this were the case, we received our classic answer, "It depends." It turned out that in some cases only these exact matches were required, but in others the inverse exchange rate (converting from Australian dollars to U.S. dollars) or an intermediate currency (going from U.S. dollars to Canadian dollars and then from Canadian dollars to Australian dollars) can be used. Which algorithm should be used varies depending on a number of things, including the company's policy and legal requirements. Thus the "It depends" hint led us to provide an extension point for deciding how to calculate exchange rates.

Related Patterns

- Innocent Questions (Section 3.2)—often the best way to identify extension points is by asking the right questions of domain experts.
- Tor's Second Cousin (Section 4.2)—sometimes points of variability identified by domain experts introduce too much complexity and should be left out of the requirements.
- Missed It by That Much (Section 6.2)—be wary of overusing patterns when they aren't appropriate, thus adding excessive complexity to the framework.

4.2 Tor's Second Cousin

Also Known As

How Extreme Is Too Extreme?

Intent

Beware of extreme requirements that unnecessarily increase framework complexity. Consider using humor to explore, refine, and evaluate the extreme requirement so it can be handled appropriately (perhaps by incorporating the requirement partially or fully into the framework, or perhaps by excluding it because of its extreme demands on framework flexibility).

Context

How would you react if, when you sat down at a restaurant table, your waiter offered you the opportunity to make your own bread, specifying exactly the combinations of different grains and other ingredients that you would like? While the rare individual might appreciate this much flexibility (and have the time to wait while the bread he or she specified was being baked), the vast majority of diners wouldn't be interested at all in such a flexible approach to restaurant bread. While this is clearly an extreme example, it raises an important question: how much flexibility within a framework is too much? When does a requirement become so extreme that it should be excluded from the framework? As usual, there are no clear-cut answers—what appears to be a reasonable and expected behavior from the perspective of one domain expert is viewed by another expert as quite far-fetched.

At first, you might think that you should err on the side of flexibility and include every possible variation that your domain experts can imagine. But if you follow this path too far, you will soon realize that your framework becomes at best very difficult to work with and at worst an incomprehensible tangle of interrelated classes and dependencies. We've found through experience that it's quite important to limit framework flexibility to a central core. Ideally this central core should be supported through a limited set of extensibility approaches, as we discuss in the Consistency Czar pattern (see Section 8.3). Users of the framework can then more easily grasp how to use the framework and rapidly take advantage of its flexibility while still preserving the ability to incorporate unusual requirements through their own extensions.

Example

In our clothing case study we discuss as one of the core requirements how and when clothing should be repaired when damaged. In some instances we might decide to discard a piece of clothing because it is too damaged to be repaired or because the repair would cost too much. Other times we might have multiple options to choose when repairing the clothing, with varying costs and resulting quality of repair.

One of our domain experts likes to weave as a hobby. This domain expert doesn't see the need to ever throw away a piece of clothing made of fabric because he can always weave a repair into the fabric so well that it can't be detected. In fact, making the repair invisible is what makes the hobby fun and challenging to him. He has also incorporated weaving support into prior clothing applications based on special customer requests. Thus, he suggests that our clothing framework provide a weaving selection algorithm that helps the clothing wearer choose the correct type of yarn or thread (color, material, thickness, and other attributes) with direct connections to all the yarn and thread suppliers so that the proper material can be automatically ordered, as well as the correct loom to use when weaving the replacement fabric.

Problem

A domain person who is very familiar with a business process can quite easily come up with many variations to that process. A framework developer needs to determine which of these variations are broadly applicable and which are so extreme that they should be excluded from the framework.

Approaches

As we mentioned in Chapter 1, software development (and framework development in particular) is a social as well as an analytical process. It's important to allow for free development and interchange of ideas during the requirements gathering stage to ensure that the resulting framework is flexible enough to be useful to a wide audience. But merely taking every idea and incorporating it as a requirement is a bad strategy—soon your requirements will become so diverse that they will be unmanageable, and if you try to implement a framework that supports those requirements, your resulting design will soon go out of control.

So how can you question what seems to be an extreme requirement without stifling good ideas in the future? Quite often, a domain expert on your team might be very good at "thinking outside of the box" and coming up with what on the surface appear to be extreme requirements. Sometimes those requirements are in fact extreme and should be left out of the framework, but other times they might describe an important point that has been overlooked by others. At the very least they can serve as a trigger for discussions that result in a significant improvement to the framework you are building. If you continually challenge requirements coming from this expert, you may make him or her less willing to voice the next idea that comes along.

We're strong believers in incorporating humor into the workplace to reduce tensions and smooth interactions among coworkers. The Tor's Second Cousin pattern uses a humorous approach to questioning extreme requirements. Tor was a very experienced and creative domain expert on the IBM SanFrancisco frameworks development team who had a knack for defining extreme requirements (usually because some application user with whom he had worked in the past wanted to do something that couldn't be done with the application). We started to jokingly blame Tor's crazy (and fictitious) second cousin for coming up with these requirements because we "knew" that "no sane person would ever want to do that." This in itself was an absurd concept, which got people in the group discussing what this crazy cousin looked like, where he lived, what he did in his spare time, and so on. We all were able to have a good laugh about this, and it allowed us to put some space between the initial challenge of the requirement and its further investigation (to see if the requirement really was extreme). Eventually Tor's second cousin got invoked for some of the ideas from most of the domain experts in the group, and this reference quickly became a simple way to kick off a constructive discussion about a potentially extreme requirement without offending the person who came up with that requirement or putting him or her into a defensive position. Sometimes we rejected the requirement as too extreme. Sometimes we accepted the requirement, perhaps in modified form, and absorbed it into our "bag of tricks" for later use, identifying a point of consistency across framework requirements (see the Consistency Is King pattern, Section 3.4). These points of consistency sometimes became the core of newly defined patterns.

Even if humor is not appropriate for your particular situation, you still need to evaluate seemingly extreme requirements. Simply accepting such requirements is not an option. In these situations it may be necessary to use an outside party, such as the domain lead or the technical lead, to initiate the discussion with the individual domain person or the domain team.

Returning back to our case study, the requirement for incorporating weaving support into our clothing framework is a natural place to invoke Tor's second cousin. While this requirement may have seemed obvious to our domain expert who weaves as a hobby, most users of our clothing framework don't enjoy weaving, so we would be making the framework overly complex by adding weaving support. However, after we've had a good laugh about some of the wild patterns Tor's second cousin must come up with when he weaves, we can have a serious discussion about how to allow for different repair choices in the framework, perhaps including the ability to closely match the original piece of clothing as a way to evaluate whether a repair should be considered (something we hadn't thought of until the perfectly matched woven repair was mentioned).

Solution

- Question and evaluate requirements that seem extreme.
- Be sensitive to the social aspects of the team.
  - Humor can be an effective way to defuse tensions when questioning unusual requirements.
  - Using an outside party may also be appropriate.

- Regardless of the approach, make sure that people have a chance to back away from the original question to gain some perspective. Knee-jerk reactions can often be defensive and can force a confrontational rather than a collaborative atmosphere.
- Don't simply discount extreme requirements. Use them as a way to explore what the framework should and shouldn't do.

When to Use/Not Use

Most people can appreciate the humor in a situation and are quite willing to participate in an "inside joke" of this type, especially when the humor is light-hearted and can't be perceived as malicious or aggressive. If handled well, this type of humor can become part of the "office lore" that helps to build up a team and quickly incorporate new members into that team. However, there are persons who have a serious nature and for whom this approach might not be appropriate. Be sensitive when trying this approach the first few times within a group so that you can begin to gauge which people will be receptive.

One of the best ways to introduce this type of humor is to initially use it against yourself in a self-deprecatory manner—this helps reassure others that you are not being malicious or aggressive. Making sure that everyone in the group is an occasional target is also helpful for preventing specific individuals from feeling singled out.

Applicability

- Consider people's personalities when using humor to question extreme requirements. Some people are not receptive to humorous interactions—try to observe an individual's day-to-day interactions with others on the team to gauge the appropriateness of this approach for that individual.
- Use this type of humor against yourself first since it will allow the group to become comfortable with the approach.
- Make sure that most people within the group are occasional targets of this type of humor to avoid the perception of bias against specific people.

Known Uses

As you might expect, we came up with quite a few extreme requirements during the development of the IBM SanFrancisco frameworks. One example involved defining a multilayer list-generation process that supported preselection of items (such as goods to be picked from a warehouse) into a candidate run list, which then were partitioned into the final lists to be used during list processing.

One typical example of this scenario is the process of generating pick lists from orders. Each order consists of order lines, one for each product in the order. A pick list is a list of products, their zones and locations within the warehouse, and the quantities needed to fill the orders. When picking is done manually, the pick list is used by a person to walk around the warehouse and pick up the amount of product specified. When generating a pick list, a number of order lines (which may be from multiple orders) for one product are consolidated into pick list details that form an entry on a pick list. One or more pick lists are generated based on different criteria, such as the zones in the warehouse and the number of people available to do picking.

Figure 4.1 shows an example of three orders being used to generate two pick lists. Order 1 consists of two order lines, one for sugar and the other for flour. Each order line indicates the product (for example, sugar), the zone in the warehouse to get it from (dry goods), the location in that zone (bin 12), and the quantity ordered (2). If we generate pick lists for all but the second order line in Order 2, based on zone, we end up with two pick lists. The first pick list consists of two pick list details, one for sugar and one for flour. The pick list

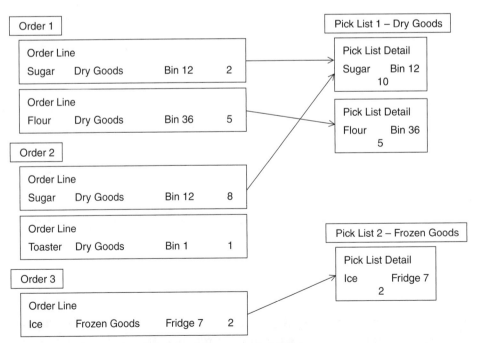

Figure 4.1   *Three orders being used to generate pick lists*

detail consists of the product (for example, sugar), the location (bin 12) and the quantity to get (10). For this first pick list detail the quantity is 10 because Order 1's order line for sugar (2) and Order 2's order line for sugar (8) can be combined.

Tor's requirements were that the framework provide two processes: one to first determine which order lines to pick (deciding to omit Order 2's order line for the toaster), followed by another that took the selected lines (a picking run) and generated the pick lists from them.

This leads to the design shown in Figure 4.2. This design consists of a PickingRun, which is the list of OrderLines to be processed. These OrderLines are chosen by the PickingRunGenerationPolicy[5]—deciding to omit Order 2's order line for the toaster. The PickingRunController manages the PickingRuns and is where you would go to initiate the generation of a PickingRun (by passing the Orders to consider). Once a PickingRun is generated it is passed to the PickListController's generatePickLists method. This method delegates to the PickListGenerationPolicy, which generates the PickLists and their associated PickListDetails—generating one pick list per zone.

After we accused Tor's second cousin of having too much time on his hands, we soon came to the conclusion that the principles behind Tor's requirement

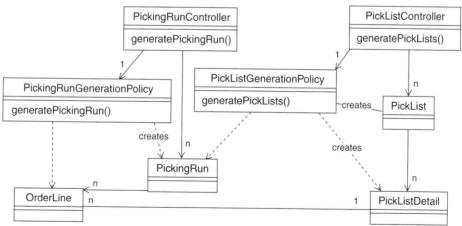

Figure 4.2 *Extreme requirement design*

---

5. Policy classes encapsulate algorithms for easy replacement. They are similar to Strategy classes as discussed in the *Design Patterns* book [Gamma 94]. Policies are described in detail in the *SanFrancisco Design Patterns* book [Carey 00, p. 61].

were sound but that a single-layer process was sufficient for the vast majority of framework users. Although in some cases the initial selection of order lines (the PickingRunGenerationPolicy) is needed, in most cases it isn't. Including this in the framework would require users who didn't need it to have to understand and, in most cases, decide to ignore it. For those few cases where it is needed it can easily be added on top of the single layer. Omitting this extreme requirement allowed us to simplify the design, shown in Figure 4.3.[6]

Related Patterns

- Consistency Is King (Section 3.4)—sometimes a seemingly extreme requirement is legitimate; these extreme requirements may need to be standardized (perhaps even to the point of defining new patterns) and applied across multiple similar domain scenarios.
- Consistency Czar (Section 8.3)—documenting consistent approaches to domain scenarios and educating team members on these approaches is crucial to ensuring the framework is understandable and predictable.

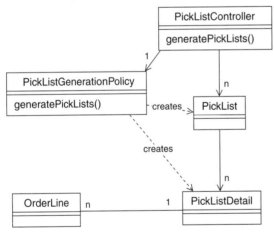

Figure 4.3 *Design after omitting the extreme requirement*

---

6. The requirement to support list generation came up in a number of places as we were developing the IBM SanFrancisco frameworks, so it was identified as the List Generation pattern. Our pick list example conforms to this pattern, which is described in detail in the *SanFrancisco Design Patterns* book [Carey 00, p. 75].

4.3 What, Not How

Also Known As

Implementations Masquerading as Requirements

Intent

When evaluating requirements, make sure that those requirements aren't just describing an implementation in disguise. Take the time to fully explore the objectives behind the stated requirements; by doing so, you may discover that the real requirements behind the stated requirements can be met by simpler, more efficient, or otherwise superior implementations than those buried in the requirements as originally stated.

Context

A domain expert isn't born overnight (which is quite a relief: we won't have to deal with four-year-old logistics experts organizing more efficient flows of toys to various play areas at preschool!). Instead, domain experts develop their expertise over many years working in a specific industry. During that time, a domain expert likely will have used numerous business applications that support various business processes. It's very easy for a domain expert to internalize the implementations provided by these applications, even to the point that it completely colors the way he or she looks at the domain.

While this is quite natural and to be expected, what we have to guard against when developing a framework is the tendency of domain experts to reiterate what they have become familiar with to the exclusion of new approaches. You may have heard stories about corporations that attempted to customize and install applications to meet their companies' specific needs, spending millions of dollars in the process only to eventually come to the point of changing their internal business processes to conform to the model defined by the application rather than being able to customize the application to their processes. This is the antithesis of our objective as framework developers—we want to design our framework so that it is highly flexible and customizable. If we take our requirements verbatim from a domain expert who is very familiar with such an application, we run the risk of reimplementing that application in our framework (along with all of its restrictions and shortcomings).

Example

In our clothing case study we discuss a requirement that needs to be met by our framework: how to purchase new clothing. Suppose that our clothing purchase domain expert has worked for a large mail order clothing retailer for most of his career. This domain expert might have become so familiar with the typical mail order process of purchasing clothes that he is unable to think about other ways that clothing can be purchased. While you might think that this domain expert needs to get out more (and you'd be correct in thinking so), let's presume that such a domain expert exists and that he describes the requirements for our clothing purchasing process as follows:

1. Leaf through the current clothing catalog until you find the clothing you want to purchase.
2. Select size, color, and style as needed for each of the clothing items.
3. Fill out the order form supplied with the catalog.
4. Send the order form in the mail to the mail order house, including payment for the clothes.
5. Wait for your clothing to arrive by parcel post a few days or weeks later.
6. Try on the received clothing and return the items you don't like or that don't fit you correctly.
7. Return to step 1 if you have returned any items in step 6.

Problem

A domain expert who is very familiar with a particular business application often tends to internalize the implementation provided by that application, even to the point of describing business requirements in a way that directly matches that application. A framework developer needs to recognize when this has occurred and discover the true requirements that are hidden within the overly restrictive process laid out by the expert.

Approaches

Returning to our example, the way the domain expert stated the requirements for clothing selection shows that he has in mind a particular implementation for purchasing clothing, that of a mail order retailer. While our expert has provided us with a good description of the process for ordering clothes from such a retailer, if we use this description as our sole requirements for clothing purchase when developing our framework, we unfortunately will rule out purchasing clothing via other approaches, such as going to a retail store, hiring a personal shopper, or going to a tailor or seamstress to order custom-made clothing. Said another way, we as framework developers need to recognize this overly restrictive set of requirements for what they are: a specific implementation tied to mail order.

Unfortunately, it's not always so obvious when implementations are imbedded within requirements. An example of this comes from our experiences developing the IBM SanFrancisco frameworks. Our accounting domain experts described as one of the core requirements for the general ledger framework the need to maintain a set of summarized balances for all accounts defined within the general ledger. While on the surface this seems to be a very reasonable requirement, as we explored it in more detail we discovered that the specific summarized balances defined in the requirement were not the only summaries that might be useful to the framework user. As we probed further, we discovered that the real requirement was to allow the user to specify which balances should be maintained.

We'll spend more time on the IBM SanFrancisco frameworks example in the Known Uses section of this chapter; we mention it here to point out that seemingly well thought out requirements statements can be implicitly tied to implementations that aren't necessarily the best way to meet the true requirements behind those statements. The only way we can determine that this is the case is to ask the domain experts questions about the domain. Usually these should take the form of "what if" questions—in effect, we are proposing additional requirements back to the domain experts to see if the requirements are valid. In our clothing purchase example above, we might ask innocent questions (see Section 3.2) such as:

- What if the user wants to purchase clothes at a retail store?
- How can this requirements scenario be adapted to support custom-made clothing purchases?

Our purpose in asking these types of questions is not to irritate the domain expert; instead, we are trying to bump him out of the rut he has formed in his brain because of his great familiarity with one specific implementation approach. Some domain experts may quickly recognize what you are doing by asking such questions and rapidly step back from their implementation view, especially if you have worked extensively with them in the past; others may see this type of question as intrusive or questioning of their knowledge of the domain or their authority as domain experts. Obviously, the first reaction makes life easier for both you and the domain experts with whom you are working, and you will find over time that most domain experts will come to appreciate these types of questions. If you encounter a domain expert who reacts badly to this type of questioning, you may need to evaluate your approach with this particular person. Perhaps you need to allow someone else who has a closer working relationship with the domain expert to ask these types of questions, or perhaps you will need to acknowledge his or her domain knowledge in the process of asking your questions. (For example, "I can see from this description that you know a great deal about mail order systems—can you point out some of the subtleties in this scenario? How can we adapt this scenario to support both mail order and retail clothing purchases?") The last thing you want to do is make an enemy of this person since you are likely going to have to work with him or her in the future, so be sensitive in the approach you take when questioning domain requirements.

You also need to be aware of a reaction possible from the opposite personality type—a domain expert who is too easily influenced by a figure of such obvious intelligence, foresight, and wisdom as yourself. Such a domain expert might too readily accept your challenge to the requirements as currently stated, when in fact those requirements do accurately state the needs of the business. For such people, you may need to frequently reassure them that you are merely asking questions and that they are the domain experts—you are just trying to learn as much as possible about the requirements before you design an approach to support them.

Once you and the domain expert recognize that you have an overly restrictive set of requirements, you then need to work together to understand the real requirements behind what has been initially written down. The "what if" questions that you have already asked lay the groundwork for building up the true requirements (or at least a closer approximation to the true requirements), so they are a natural starting point for discovering unnecessary restrictions or assumptions. In most cases, the domain expert will need to spend some time thinking about these restrictions and proposing a new set of requirements that avoid them. Sometimes this will lead the expert to identify a new extension point (see the It Depends pattern, Section 4.1) that he or she otherwise would not have documented in the requirements. You've done your job by alerting the domain expert to the restrictions; now let him or her complete the cycle by refining the requirements. You might have to iterate through this cycle a few times before you are both happy with the end results, and you should also make sure that other domain experts (including the lead expert or at least a senior member of the domain team) validate the final requirements (see the Alles in Ordnung pattern, Section 3.1).

Solution

- Question and evaluate requirements that appear to be too tightly tied to implementations.
- Use "what if" types of questions to point out potential areas where overly restrictive requirements exist.
- Be sensitive to the personality type of the domain expert when asking questions.
  - Reassure domain experts who feel their knowledge is being challenged that you do respect their domain knowledge and expertise.
  - Remind less confident or less assertive domain experts that you are not a domain expert and that they should treat your comments as questions and not statements of correctness.
- Once both you and the domain expert recognize that implementation details are present in the requirements as currently stated, give the domain expert time to reformulate the requirements to eliminate those implementation details.
- Expect to iterate on requirements to get them correct.
- Involve other domain experts as part of the process to validate and assist in reformulating requirements where needed.

When to Use/Not Use

If you believe that implementation details are present in and significantly affect a requirements statement, you need to question those details, either directly or indirectly. Sometimes the implementation details present in a statement are so insignificant as to be immaterial to the requirements as stated. Other times, the implementation described in the requirements statement may be the most natural approach to implementing the requirements, or the requirements area is so well understood that everyone agrees on the desired implementation approach. In these cases, you need to assess the risk of an overly restrictive design against the need to focus on other, less stable or less understood portions of the overall framework requirements.

Applicability

- Implementation details are likely to be present in most requirements statements to some degree.
- Pick the most important and highest risk aspects of your framework to focus on when applying this rule. As you evaluate these aspects of your

requirements, consider the specific requirement you are evaluating in the context of other requirements statements since these may affect your viewpoint.

Known Uses

This pattern broadly applies to software development in general. Good software development should avoid remaking the mistakes of the past. Recognizing that past implementations can easily creep into new requirements statements is an important step in this process.

As we worked with the domain experts who defined the requirements for the IBM SanFrancisco frameworks, we discovered over time that, since many of our domain experts had not only defined the requirements for other business applications but had also written the software for some of those applications, the domain experts were susceptible to including their past implementations in their requirements statements. Over time, the experts themselves became more and more aware of this tendency, and by the time we were working on a later set of framework requirements, they were quite good at preventing implementations from creeping into requirements statements.

Returning to our specific IBM SanFrancisco frameworks example of summarized balances above, if we'd accepted the original requirements as stated, we would have created a framework with a fixed set of balances—the balance of each account for each period—and users would have been able to retrieve only those balances.

Instead, the types of questions we asked as frameworks designers included the following.

- What if users aren't interested in the summarized balances listed in the requirements statement—should they be able to turn off those balances?
- What if users want to look at summaries that aren't covered by the requirements statement? Do users have to hand-calculate those balances, or should the framework be able to calculate those balances for them?

These types of questions were sufficient to get our domain experts thinking about their requirements more broadly than the requirements as they were originally proposed and documented. With these "true" requirements we were able to provide an implementation that fulfilled the original requirements (by allowing balances to be kept for each account for each period) and fulfilled the new requirements by giving the user control of what balances are kept and using the balances for as many requests as possible.

Related Patterns

- Alles in Ordnung (Section 3.1)—use the checkpoints built into your development process as a final validation that the requirements as stated are truly requirements.

- Innocent Questions (Section 3.2)—follow suggested guidelines for how to ask questions that probe requirements.

- It Depends (Section 4.1)—sometimes uncovering an implicit implementation in a requirements statement will ultimately transform that portion of the statement into an extension point.

4.4 The Stupid Test

Also Known As

Include Obvious Domain Capabilities While Keeping the Framework Focused

Intent

In most cases, when a framework doesn't make direct use of a potential attribute or behavior (in other words, the domain processes built into the framework don't depend on a potential framework element to complete their work), it's best to not include that capability within the framework. However, if the element in question is very likely to be used by applications built from the framework, consider including that element even though the framework doesn't directly use it.

Context

How many features does your cell phone have? And how many of those features do you use on a day-to-day basis? Can you even remember how to use most of the capabilities of your cell phone? While most cell phone manufacturers have improved ease of use for their latest products, many designers of early cell phones succumbed to the temptation to provide everything for everyone, often through bewilderingly complex keystroke combinations. We have to confront the same issues when building a framework, striking a balance between meeting most potential uses of the framework and keeping the framework simple. Trying to make the framework useful in more situations causes additional framework complexity, while simplifying the framework can make it too restrictive to use in typical environments. We might be able to think of lots of different capabilities that could be useful to users of our framework, but if we add too many of these behaviors or attributes to the framework's objects, we risk making the framework so hard to understand that users will become frustrated or make mistakes when using the framework (see the It Depends pattern, Section 4.1, and the Tor's Second Cousin pattern, Section 4.2).

One useful guideline when considering whether to add a capability to the framework is to check if other parts of the framework place a dependency on the capability under consideration. If such dependencies exist, there is good reason to incorporate the new behavior or attribute. But what if there isn't a dependency on this capability within the framework? This is where we need to apply the "stupid test"—will the framework look stupid to a potential user if it doesn't provide this capability?

Example

Let's consider how clothing repair is handled within our case study. We indicated in Chapter 2 that the process for repairing clothes needs to be customizable. One of the more typical clothing failure incidents is the well-known and dreaded lost button scenario. Since buttons are present on many articles of clothing, we could decide to add attributes to our clothing base class that are used to describe button characteristics (for example, size, shape, manufacturer). Let's also suppose that we have defined a clothing class hierarchy, with various classes such as shirts, pants, and socks, defined as subclasses under the clothing base class. With this hierarchy in place, we could also decide to place these button description attributes to only those subclasses where buttons are most likely to be present—it doesn't make a lot of sense to talk about buttons on socks (unless we are working with Japanese geisha socks, which button up the back), but it might make more sense to add these attributes to a shirt subclass. How do we decide where to place these attributes (if anywhere) in the framework?

Problem

There are many possibilities to consider when defining the core capabilities of a framework. A framework developer must decide which capabilities to include in the framework, including some capabilities that aren't directly used within the framework. How do you decide which capabilities to include?

Approaches

We want to avoid cluttering our framework with capabilities that will be rarely used, but not to the extent of making the framework so sparsely populated that it becomes difficult to use. In other words, we want our framework classes to look "natural" to a business analyst familiar with the framework's domain who is looking at our framework for the first time.

This is the essence of the stupid test—make sure that the framework has all the capabilities that a reasonable domain expert would expect to have provided by the framework. Returning to our example, we can use the stupid test to evaluate our placement of button description attributes throughout our clothing class hierarchy. A domain expert would not reasonably expect to see these attributes present on the clothing base class, nor on most of the subclasses we describe. Even though there might be isolated situations where these attributes would be useful (like our geisha socks case), these attributes would not be useful or helpful in the general case—they don't pass the stupid test.

When we get to the shirt class, however, we might come to a different conclusion. Many shirts have buttons, and we might decide that they are common enough to warrant adding these attributes to the shirt class.[7] Looking at each of the attributes, we would probably all agree that the size and color attributes are generally useful—they pass the stupid test. However, we will probably come to a different conclusion for the manufacturer attribute. Unless the clothing is very specialized or very expensive, it's unlikely that our repair algorithms need information about the original button manufacturer. We are better off not including this attribute in the framework since it's unlikely to be used.

Solution

- When considering framework capabilities that aren't directly used by other aspects of the framework, evaluate their likely use within applications built from the framework.
- If the framework will look stupid to a domain expert without the capability under consideration, this is a good indication that the attribute or behavior should be included in the framework.

---

7. You may argue that there are plenty of shirts that don't use buttons, and you'd be correct. If our example bothers you to the point of distraction, add a collared shirt subclass to your clothing class hierarchy and resume with the example.

- Be cautious about adding too many capabilities under this rule. It is very easy to add clutter to a framework, making the framework more cumbersome to use.

When to Use/Not Use

Use this rule whenever a proposed framework capability isn't obviously required by the framework. In general, this rule applies more to framework attributes than behaviors. It's not likely that a domain expert will specify an unused behavior as part of the requirements; on the other hand, adding a list of attributes otherwise unused within the framework is much more likely to occur. Your domain team is the best judge of whether the proposed capabilities are natural aspects of the domain (and thus should be included in the framework).

Adding an unneeded attribute to a framework doesn't simply mean adding an insignificant detail to the framework's object model. Each additional attribute has three effects that can cause problems.

1. It creates more for the users of the class to understand, especially when it is an attribute they do not need in their domain. They will spend time trying to figure out what they should (or shouldn't) do with the unrecognized attribute.

2. It creates more for the persistence layer to support. Some persistence layers are flexible enough to support not using a column for an attribute, instead returning a default null value. However, if this attribute is defined as mandatory, taking this approach can be done only after you have determined that none of the framework code you are using is dependent on that value.

3. It creates more work for someone extending (that is, subclassing) the class. That person now needs to understand what the attribute is and figure out how the extension can support it or needs to determine that it is unused and can be ignored by the extension.

Applicability

- Consider applying this rule to classes that have potentially many domain attributes.
- Occasionally, you may find it useful to apply this rule to class behavior as well.

Known Uses

We used this rule during the development of the IBM SanFrancisco frameworks primarily to add attributes throughout various business objects in the frameworks. One typical attribute that we added throughout numerous Entity classes is Address, even though it was rarely used in framework algorithms. We also added various capacity-related attributes to the warehouse management framework's StockLocation class (used to represent a physical position in a warehouse), even though the default stock putaway algorithm (determining what to put where in the warehouse) didn't make use of those attributes. Why did we do this? Because our domain experts realized that almost all businesses use stock putaway rules that take into account the capacity of the stock location being considered.[8] Because stock putaway rules vary so greatly from deployment to deployment, it's impossible to provide a useful algorithm within the framework; however, it's also very unlikely that a framework user will be able to provide a useful algorithm without these attributes.

Related Patterns

- It Depends (Section 4.1)—the stupid test is a counterbalance to excessive flexibility that might otherwise be introduced into a framework.
- Tor's Second Cousin (Section 4.2)—discussing potentially excessive framework elements in a humorous way can lead to better decisions on the inclusion or exclusion of those elements.

---

8. One of the few exceptions occurs when the location has essentially infinite capacity with respect to the stock being stored (for example, if the stock location is a staging area on a manufacturing floor used to hold supplies of small parts for use in the manufacturing process).

Chapter

5

Analysis

If requirements are the raw materials of a framework, analysis begins the refinement process of these materials. Effective analysis identifies key entities (the "nouns" of your framework), allocates responsibilities (business processes and process fragments) extracted from framework requirements amongst those entities, and begins the process of partitioning the resulting model (typically developed using the Unified Modeling Language) into loosely coupled and separable components. The resulting models carry through key requirements concepts and terminology into a form that domain experts understand and that serves as a foundation for framework design. Patterns that will assist you in the analysis phase include

- Eating the Elephant (Section 5.1)—decomposing the framework into components

- Something Is Better Than Nothing (Section 5.2)—allocating framework responsibilities through iteration

- Where's Mr. Spock When You Need Him? (Section 5.3)—ensuring effective communication among domain and technical participants during the analysis process

We discuss these patterns in this chapter.

5.1 Eating the Elephant (One *Byte* at a Time . . .)

Also Known As

Decomposing the Problem

Intent

When analyzing the problem domain of your framework, look for opportunities to separate major aspects of your framework into components that have minimal interactions with other components. Analysis classes with high affinity to other classes should be grouped with those classes, and you should establish unidirectional relationships between those groupings to ease dependency management.

Context

If you've worked on object-oriented systems for very long, you're sure to have come across applications that are "object spaghetti"—masses of classes with no discernable organization or structure, just one huge, tangled web. Even if the developers of such systems did a good job of encapsulation within those classes, maintaining or enhancing such systems can still be quite painful because of the many cross-class dependencies that must be managed whenever any single class is modified.

Remember that one of the core objectives of object-oriented development is to isolate change. As a system is initially developed, isolating change makes it possible to develop major sections of the system independently from each other (eating the elephant one bite at a time, as the old joke goes), establishing limited interconnections between those sections. Just as important, defining a well-decomposed system makes it possible to make significant modifications to that system within a small number of classes.

Proper decomposition at the analysis level is one example of the "divide and conquer" principle discussed in Section 3.3. By "chunking" classes into clusters that have tight affinity, with each cluster establishing more loosely coupled relationships to other clusters, we enable domain analysts, designers, and developers working on the project to grasp aspects of the project a piece at a time, and in the process we establish a set of coarse-grained components that can be more easily separated and used independently of each other (see Appendix A).

Example

In our clothing case study, we identified four major aspects to include in our framework:

1. Selecting—deciding what to wear
2. Cleaning—handling the dirty laundry
3. Repairing—fixing damaged clothing
4. Purchasing—acquiring additional clothing

Consider what would occur if we didn't attempt to separate these aspects during the framework analysis process. For example, we might mix selecting clothing with purchasing new clothing because we see similarities between the two—in both cases, the user of the clothing is selecting clothing items. We might define a ClothingUser class and assign responsibility to this class to select clothes to wear and also to purchase new clothes. This class will clearly need to work closely with the ClothingItem class and probably with classes that represent places to put clothing, including the Closet class and the ClothingStore class, as shown in Figure 5.1. Before we know it, we will pull more and more analysis classes into close affinity with each other, eventually creating a very large, hard-to-understand, and difficult-to-manage analysis model. This model will become only more complex as we integrate functional and technical design aspects into our framework, and as we begin to implement our design, we will most likely discover that we need to implement a large portion of the framework all at once because of these tangled cross-class dependencies.

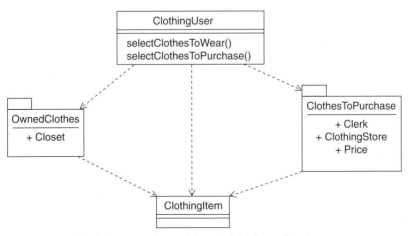

Figure 5.1 *ClothingUser class with multiple dependencies*

Problem

Analysis models can, in their initial form, blur class responsibilities and, as a result, establish tight dependencies across large numbers of analysis classes. If time isn't taken up front to clearly define (and possibly reallocate) class responsibilities and to look for reasonably sized clusters of analysis classes that have strong affinity to each other, the resulting framework is likely to be difficult to understand, use, and maintain.

Approaches

During your initial analysis work, your objective is to capture the key domain "nouns" within the framework—entities, in Jacobson's object-oriented software engineering (OOSE) terminology [Jacobson 92]—and allocate domain responsibilities to those entities. This process is by its nature iterative, and as you begin the process you will likely have at best a vague idea of how your coarse-grained framework component categories (groupings of analysis entities that have high affinity toward each other and that can present a consolidated coarse-grained interface to the outside world) should look. It's still worth attempting to lay out this set of components early and to place your analysis entities into these components. However, you won't always be able to clearly identify a component location for every one of your entities. When this happens, you have two options: (1) pick the best-fit component for your entity or (2) create a new component that better fits the entity's responsibilities. Neither approach is always the right one, and in many ways it doesn't matter which approach you choose because you're not trying to get the perfect analysis model the first time—you're just trying to capture key capabilities of your framework and get them in front of you so you can step back and look at the big picture later (see the Something Is Better Than Nothing pattern, Section 5.2).

Once you have a good portion of your entities laid out and their responsibilities tentatively assigned, you need to look at the overall layout of your entities and the dependencies established between the various categories you've initially laid out for your framework. At this stage in the analysis process, you are likely to find that some categories are as heavily populated as Hong Kong and others are as empty as the Australian outback. Now's the time to consider creating new component categories and possibly removing some of the sparsely inhabited ones. This process isn't an exact science, and you and your team are likely to get into arguments about the placement of an entity into one category or another.

You are also likely to find that some component categories have many dependencies on other categories. While not necessarily indicative of a problem, such heavy cross-component dependencies will create development and maintenance complexities for you in the future. Sometimes, however, tangled cross-component dependencies indicate that you have misplaced responsibilities. Maybe you have placed too much responsibility on one of your analysis classes and should either move some responsibilities to other classes in other components (perhaps moving the generic selection-related capabilities shared between our clothing selection and clothing purchase components from our example into a lower-level utility component) or perhaps even partition that class into two or more analysis classes with lesser scope (something we should consider doing to our ClothingUser class in our example above—see Figure 5.2). Once you've repartitioned some of your analysis classes in this way, you should be able to reduce interactions and dependencies between components.

Minimizing dependencies between components is necessary but not sufficient to build a well-decomposed and maintainable framework. You also need to make sure that the components establish only one-way dependencies with other components in the framework. What does this mean? Returning to our original analysis model in Figure 5.1, let's treat the OwnedClothes package as a coarse-grained component. In addition, let's assume that ClothingUser is contained in another higher-level coarse-grained component labeled ClothingUsers and that our requirements state that each Closet within the OwnedClothes package must maintain a reference to the ClothingUser who "owns" that closet (see Figure 5.3).

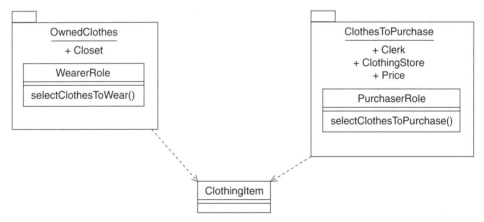

Figure 5.2   *ClothingUser class partitioned into two roles, WearerRole and PurchaserRole*

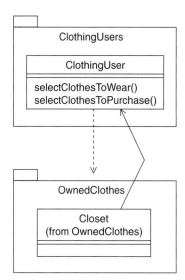

Figure 5.3   *Example of cross-component upward dependency*

While this is a trivial example, it illustrates an important point: as soon as we introduce this type of cross-component dependency, we have increased the "critical mass" of classes necessary to develop either the ClothingUsers or the OwnedClothes component because we can't develop either of these components independently of each other. This isn't an issue in the case of ClothingUsers since we expected to have a dependency on OwnedClothes, but it could become an issue for OwnedClothes, since we could reasonably expect to be able to develop this component without having to know anything about clothing users. We also have made framework maintenance more difficult because we are less likely to be able to work on one component in isolation—if we make changes to ClothingUsers in our example, we may very well affect behaviors in OwnedClothes; once we adjust OwnedClothes to take those changes into account, we could affect ClothingUsers in turn.

While this isn't an insurmountable difficulty, you should strive to eliminate two-way dependencies between your coarse-grained framework components—doing so will make your life easier in the long run. We discuss a technique using object properties that helps alleviate this type of upward dependency in the Known Uses section later in this chapter. (You may have noticed that this upward dependency issue isn't present in the refactored version of this example shown in Figure 5.2. Refactoring often helps resolve upward dependency issues such as these.)

Finally, you should evaluate each of your component categories to make sure that the amount of information contained within them is readily understandable by a typical analyst or developer. While there will always be people who can seemingly absorb the entire complexity of your framework and reproduce it in excruciating detail at will, these people are few and far between. You should strive to create component categories that introduce information in approximately 10 elements or less (the "7 ± 2" rule). Studies have shown that most people can grasp this many distinct concepts at once; going much beyond this number makes the information difficult to comprehend and absorb [Miller 56]. This isn't a hard and fast rule; if you do have a component that has a high level of complexity for a valid reason, consider defining subcomponents within the coarse-grained component that illustrate specific aspects of the component. These subcomponents can often be developed to a great extent in isolation within the context of the larger component, thus increasing the likelihood that you will be able to follow the "7 ± 2" rule for each subcomponent.

Solution

- Look for clear separation points between analysis classes, and use these points to establish large-scale component boundaries with minimal interaction between those components. You may need to move classes between large-scale component categories, move responsibilities from one class to another, or break an existing class into two or more classes to minimize coupling between coarse-grained components within your framework.
- Avoid cross-component dependencies that go in both directions, since this makes both development and maintenance of your framework more difficult.
- Try to follow the "7 ± 2" rule, grouping approximately seven related analysis classes into class clusters that can be presented to the framework designer and user in a single easy-to-understand class diagram.

When to Use/Not Use

Like most analysis techniques, component-level decomposition needs to be applied at the right time in the analysis cycle. For example, how do you know when you've done enough initial analysis to warrant stepping back? You need to strike a balance between overiterating, where you spend more time changing your model than enhancing it, and going so far into initial analysis before attempting decomposition that it becomes difficult to sort out cross-dependencies and poor entity groupings. This will vary from framework to framework, depending on its complexity, how well known and stable the domain you're analyzing is, and other factors.

You will also need to decide when you've completed enough decomposition to move on to the next stage of your analysis work. Remember that iteration is a way of life in framework development and software development in general (see the Iterate, Iterate, Iterate pattern, Section 3.5), and also remember that perfection is not required or even desirable. There will be some categories that remain somewhat sparse after decomposition and others that seem a bit crowded. Maybe these categories will sort themselves out in a later iteration, or maybe you'll decide that they're acceptable the way they are. As you complete further analysis, adding additional classes and refactoring others, the right decision is likely to become clear to you.

Applicability

- Consider component-level decomposition when analyzing any framework large enough to exceed the "7 ± 2" rule in its entirety.
- Complete the initial decomposition relatively early in the analysis phase of your development cycle.
- Continue to evaluate the decomposition level of your framework throughout the development cycle; as new analysis classes are added to the framework, unforeseen cross-component dependencies can easily be introduced, as can features defined during framework design.

Known Uses

These decomposition principles apply to any software development project involving more than a handful of developers. Good decomposition leads to cleanly decoupled software components.

We used component-level decomposition heavily throughout the IBM San-Francisco frameworks. One example of such decomposition is within the Warehouse Management Core Business Process (CBP) of the frameworks. Within this CBP, we defined a core Product component that contained the core Product and Warehouse structural definitions along with basic capabilities associated with these classes. Because these capabilities are quite extensive, the number of classes contained within this category exceeded the "7 ± 2" rule, so we further decomposed the Product component into numerous sub-components (see Figure 5.4).

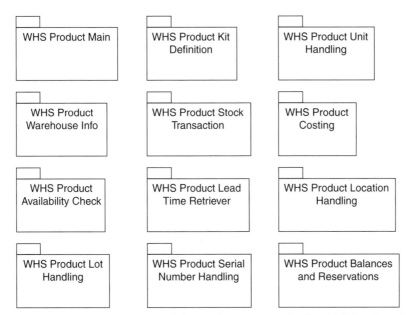

Figure 5.4 *Decomposition of the Product category in the IBM SanFrancisco frameworks*

The Warehouse Management CBP also supports numerous business processes associated with warehousing, such as picking goods from stock, receiving goods into stock, and so on (see Figure 5.5). Each of these components establishes a one-way dependency on the Product component; thus it is possible to

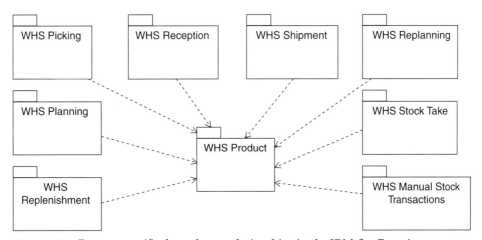

Figure 5.5 *Process-specific dependency relationships in the IBM SanFrancisco Product category*

maintain, use, or enhance any one of these components in isolation from all others in the Warehouse Management CBP.

Another example from the IBM SanFrancisco frameworks involves managing upward dependencies: our domain experts often expressed the need to be able to navigate from lower-level framework entities to higher-level entities within the framework (in other words, they wanted to establish upward dependencies between component categories). We typically resolved these situations in one of three ways.

1. Where possible, we deferred the coupling to the application developer (see the Pass the Buck pattern, Section 6.1). The application developer using the framework understands exactly what relationships are needed to meet the requirements of the application and can directly establish those relationships without establishing upward dependencies, since by definition application categories are at a higher level than framework categories.

2. In some cases, the upward relationship was valid but did not affect the behavior of the lower-level class. In these situations, we established a loosely coupled upward relationship through dynamic properties [Carey 00]. Because specific properties are not implemented as part of the class but instead added to object instances at runtime, they do not directly affect the design or implementation of the lower-level class. This allows for clean separation between categories during development and maintenance.

3. In rare cases where the coupling was both required and affected the behavior of the lower-level class, we recategorized classes to allow the establishment of the tightly coupled relationship between classes.

Related Patterns

- Divide and Conquer (Section 3.3)—in framework analysis, consider separating classes into subcomponents that can be more easily used independently of each other.

- Iterate, Iterate, Iterate (Section 3.5)—component decomposition should be done on an iterative basis.

- Something Is Better Than Nothing (Section 5.2)—when allocating analysis entities into component categories, make a best-fit attempt and don't focus on perfection.

- Pass the Buck (Section 6.1)—when defining coarse-grained components within a framework, try to defer the decision to establish coupling between these components to the user of the framework.

5.2 Something Is Better Than Nothing

Also Known As

Document What You Know When You Know It

Intent

In the early stages of analysis, it's often important to document what you know in imperfect form, sorting out the details as you iterate over the analysis model.

Context

How many times have you thought of something you needed to do but didn't write it down, then forgot what it was five minutes later? It's easy to lose track of information amidst all the distractions that arise every day. Not surprisingly, we have to deal with these same issues during software development. Information not gathered when first encountered is often lost and must be rediscovered later. Rather than taking the chance of losing this information, it's better to place it somewhere, even if it is in the wrong place or format.

This piece of common sense is not always easy to follow. It becomes especially difficult when doing framework analysis. During analysis, we are not only fighting the quantity of information but also the interactions between the domain experts and the technical experts. The bulk of the initial analysis is done by the domain experts. Normally they are not object-oriented analysis experts. They typically get a short, informal education session and then are supported by one of the technical experts, since the technical team is often still working on the previous release or project and thus is unable to give full attention to analysis work.

This creates a problem, since some domain experts believe they are experts at analysis and others believe they aren't. Those who do are like many people new to object-oriented design: they often create abstractions where abstractions aren't appropriate. Those who don't are often afraid to add things to the model for fear of making mistakes—possibly talking to others about their ideas and assuming someone else will put the ideas in the model if needed. There is no malice in these actions, and some are even unconscious. The domain experts are just trying to make the analysis model the best it can be with the skills they have.

In addition, as domain experts work together, many things may be unspoken—those aspects of the analysis that are obvious to anyone familiar with the domain. Domain experts aren't always programmers (or used to working with programmers), and as a result they may not have been initiated into a world where everything, no matter how trivial, has to be written down or it won't appear in the end product.

As long as everything is captured somewhere in the analysis model, we can move analysis classes, refactor classes, or otherwise modify our model as we iterate (as described in the Eating the Elephant pattern, Section 5.1). As a result we will have an analysis model that represents more completely our objectives.

Example

Our example from the Eating the Elephant pattern suits our purposes here as well. Remember from that example that we initially defined a ClothingUser class that had responsibilities for selecting clothes both to wear and to purchase. As our domain experts created this initial model, they suppressed the urge to overanalyze the situation (which could easily have resulted in excessive partitioning of function), and they managed to include the "obvious" or otherwise unspoken elements of clothing handling, like the need to store owned clothes in a closet. The end result was a very reasonable starting point for our analysis. However, we eventually discovered that this approach unnecessarily coupled two otherwise independent aspects of the framework, so we split the ClosingUser class into two new classes representing the Wearer and Purchaser roles of a clothing user.

Problem

Initial analysis models are normally less than ideal. Domain experts focusing on perfecting the model too early in the analysis process leads to loss of important information.

Approaches

There are many techniques for capturing information and, in most cases, you can use whatever is appropriate for you. For analysis, with its unique problems, we suggest following a standard object-oriented analysis approach. Approaches such as CRC (Class-Responsibility-Collaboration) [Booch 94] and noun identification in use cases [Jacobson 92] are very useful in the initial stages of analysis modeling. Having a clearly defined way to capture this information and clearly identifying that the domain team is responsible for its capture (thereby avoiding contention between domain experts and designers and avoiding the concern that "the OO experts are looking over my shoulder so I'd better not make any mistakes") is crucial.

Equally as crucial is making sure that the domain team knows that you don't expect them to produce the final analysis model. They need to understand that the initial analysis is about capturing as much information as possible; they are setting the stage for further analysis and that through iteration the final analysis model will be achieved. In other words, make sure they know they don't have to get it right the first time—it doesn't have to be perfect.

Encourage your domain experts to not overlook the obvious attributes and behaviors that might not otherwise be documented as part of the framework requirements (see The Stupid Test pattern, Section 4.4). Especially during this initial analysis, they shouldn't spend too much time focusing on ideal class definitions and attribute and behavior placement. While you should make an effort to help your experts place information appropriately, beyond a certain level this effort will become counterproductive. If your experts want to create abstractions, ask that they document what went into the abstraction and why they thought it was interesting. If they have attributes to add but don't know where to put them, they should place those attributes based on their best judgment.

Don't get hung up on getting things exactly right at this point. Remember that as you continue to develop the analysis model through iteration (see the Iterate, Iterate, Iterate pattern, Section 3.5), you are likely to make changes to already developed aspects regardless of how much time you initially spent on them, not to mention the likelihood that the requirements driving your analysis model are going to change even before you complete your first release! It is crucial that you keep this in mind. Don't paralyze the domain experts by making them wary of adding incorrect things or making the model wrong. As a developer supporting this initial capture, ensure that you make it clear to your domain experts that you don't know the domain and your questions are not challenges or statements of direction (see the Innocent Questions pattern, Section 3.2). Also, resist the temptation to refine the model during initial capture. Let this first pass run to completion before you distract the domain experts with the finer points of object-oriented analysis techniques. (Some of your domain experts may be interested in learning more about object-oriented analysis. While this is a laudable goal, diving too deeply into this education can easily distract the team from its primary objective—to rapidly flesh out a useful first-pass analysis model. As the model is refined, these domain experts can then gain experience in the subtleties of object-oriented analysis without slowing down the project or engaging in needless "navel-gazing" over model elements that are likely to be changed in the future.)

As you begin to iterate against your first-pass analysis model, you will undoubtedly make changes to it. You may discover that you have overspecified your analysis model, putting too much information into its various classes. Or you may have included redundant information, either because different teams developed different aspects of the analysis model independently or because you realize that what you thought were two distinct concepts should be abstracted or otherwise merged (see the Eating the Elephant pattern, Section 5.1). We've found it helpful when encountering this situation to temporarily move the pruned information into a "recycling bin" category within the analysis model. This gives you time to consider your change and allows you the flexibility to recover the pruned information with minimal effort should you change your mind at a later point.

Solution

- Have a clear process for developing your analysis model as well as clearly defined responsibilities and ownership within that process.
  - Consider techniques such as CRC cards and noun identification in use cases.
  - Clearly place responsibility on the domain experts for defining the initial model and on the design team to work with these experts to refine the model.
- In the early stages of model analysis, focus on documenting all that you know about the domain.
  - Don't focus on perfection—expect the model to change as you iterate and extend it.
  - Remember to document the "obvious" elements of the model that domain experts might not explicitly describe or document in their requirements.
- As the model matures, look for opportunities to improve it.
  - Group classes and behaviors based on affinity (see the Eating the Elephant pattern, Section 5.1).
  - Prune model elements that are redundant or extraneous or that otherwise clutter the model (see The Stupid Test pattern, Section 4.4).
  - Place the pruned information in a staging-ground portion of the model for awhile to make sure that it really is appropriate to remove that information from the model.

When to Use/Not Use

As the domain problem being addressed becomes more complex, the need becomes greater for documenting what you know about the domain when you know it. Simple domains can often be analyzed quickly and completely (although overconfidence when doing this analysis can lead to significant mistakes), while complex domains often lead to subtle abstractions and groupings that aren't evident during the early stages of analysis.

Also, even when the domain expert and the technical expert are the same person, we have found that it is better to complete a quick initial pass of the analysis model—a pass that captures as much as possible—returning to refine the analysis model during a later iteration.

Applicability

- Iteration and rapid prototyping are core to our development philosophy, and this pattern is merely one aspect of this iterative approach to development. We believe that "hitting the enter key" (in other words, a bias toward action rather than introspection) is the best way to learn about a framework, both what works and what needs to be changed.

Known Uses

As you might expect, this pattern broadly applies in all aspects of software development. Taking a first pass through the problem domain and implementing that pass as a prototype or initial product release (as recommended by most modern software engineering development processes) teaches you much more than a longer and more drawn-out analysis process.

Within the IBM SanFrancisco frameworks, we typically asked our domain experts to define the initial analysis model for a particular domain aspect, followed by an initial iteration completed by a technical developer in parallel with a domain expert. This first combined pass was usually sufficient to provide a model that could be used as a starting point for initial design, with that design work often leading to additional iterations in the associated analysis model.

Related Patterns

- Innocent Questions (Section 3.2)—make sure that developers supporting the creation of the initial analysis model by domain experts clearly state that their questions to the domain experts are meant only to help the developers explore and learn the domain.
- Iterate, Iterate, Iterate (Section 3.5)—iterations are likely to change the analysis model, so don't be overly concerned about initial perfection.

- The Stupid Test (Section 4.4)—encourage domain experts to not overlook the obvious attributes and behaviors that might not otherwise be documented as part of the framework requirements.
- Eating the Elephant (Section 5.1)—capture what you know now as part of the problem decomposition process.

5.3 Where's Mr. Spock When You Need Him?

Also Known As

Domain–Technical Cross-Team Communication

Intent

Framework developers need in-depth information about the domain functions for which they have responsibility. The earlier this information can be transferred, the less likely that functional errors will be introduced, and those errors that are introduced will be less costly to correct.

Context

The first point in the development process where the domain and technical teams typically work closely together is on the analysis model. If pains aren't taken to transfer domain information to designers during the analysis stage, those designers will be very likely to miss important concepts when designing and implementing the framework. This information transfer needs to occur both within the output of the analysis stage (the analysis model itself) and in the heads of the framework designers since they must be able to put this model in context as they proceed with design. Without the help of Mr. Spock's Vulcan mind-meld (or a reasonable facsimile thereof), this level of knowledge transfer won't happen automatically. Since there aren't many Vulcans involved in software development (at least we aren't aware of any—although come to think of it . . .), we need to come up with different information transfer techniques.

Example

Anyone who has watched software developers leaving work knows that a strong fashion sense isn't a requirement to develop software. In our case study, it's particularly important that our framework designers gain some understanding of clothing fashion rules and guidelines (or at least get some sense of what styles, colors, and patterns of clothing normally go together). Otherwise, the selection portion of our framework might be designed without sufficient flexibility to support various styles of dress, or even worse, it might allow framework users to make serious fashion errors such as mixing stripes and plaids (in other words, to dress like software developers).

Problem

While developers don't need to become experts in the domain, they need to gain at least a basic understanding of it and will likely need to develop a deeper understanding of domain topics and issues in the specific areas of domain function for which they are responsible.

Approaches

We've found it very helpful for domain experts to begin the process of transferring domain information by defining an initial analysis model. Even though this model is likely to contain many errors, it still provides a useful base to which the technical team can apply their analysis skills. Ideally, before beginning this work, at least one member of the domain team should have prior experience in object-oriented modeling so the domain team can avoid fundamental modeling errors in its work. In any event, make sure that one of your best analysis modelers from the technical team participates in this initial modeling process, both as a mentor to teach good modeling techniques and as an initial validator of the modeling work done by the domain team (lightly reviewing the model for completeness and not focusing on model refinement, as described in the Something Is Better Than Nothing pattern, Section 5.2). If this technical person can also play the role of the great communicator (see The Great Communicator pattern, Section 8.2), all the better, since he or she will be able to absorb a great deal of domain knowledge through the mentoring process.

Be careful if many of your domain experts have prior data modeling experience. This "data-up" approach usually results in analysis models in which the domain data is decoupled from behavior—in essence, a procedural approach that doesn't incorporate important object-oriented principles such as data encapsulation. If you aren't aware of this, such an approach can easily seep into the analysis and design, requiring additional rework late in the development cycle.

Once the initial analysis model has been established, effective communication between domain and technical experts is essential to refining that model. You could start with the most crisply and completely defined requirements ever put to paper, but if your technical experts are unable to understand the implications of those requirements, they are likely to misallocate responsibilities across analysis classes, even to the point of completely dropping some requirements from the resulting implementation.

We've found that we need to use different techniques to establish this communication. High-level model walk-throughs led by domain experts are very useful for getting the entire team to discuss and understand basic domain concepts. Once everyone has participated in this walk-through, allow designers to proceed with their education in the ways that are most comfortable for them. Some designers prefer a primarily self-study approach, while others want further detailed walk-through sessions.

As designers become more comfortable with the initial model, they begin to naturally make adjustments to the model. This refinement process is crucial to building a complete and accurate analysis model. A one-on-one approach works best during this stage of analysis model development, with pairs of domain experts and designers given responsibility for various portions of the framework. As you might expect, your domain experts have an important responsibility here, asking the necessary innocent questions to ensure that all requirements make the transition into the analysis model (see the Innocent Questions pattern, Section 3.2). In many cases, the original analysis model triggers these questions, since its contents are a type of domain checklist. If a concept captured in the original analysis model isn't present in the refined model, this mismatch becomes an obvious point of discussion. The domain expert's participation can also help ensure that the analysis model continues to focus on analysis and does not creep into design.

At some point, the analysis model is deemed complete enough to continue with design, at least for this development iteration. As we mentioned in the Alles in Ordnung pattern (see Section 3.1), every development process should have well-defined checkpoints established at points in the process where crucial decisions are being made and where it would be painful to have to reverse course. Such checkpoints not only allow team leaders to validate the work already completed but also give them a chance to gauge the level of information transfer that has occurred between domain and technical team members. Some teams might not be as effective as others in communicating with each other, and these teams might need special attention along the way. In the worst case, you may need to restructure teams to avoid communication or personality problems—this should be a last resort, however, since each team has already invested quite a bit of time establishing a working relationship (see the There Is No "I" in Team pattern, Section 8.1).

Depending on the composition of your team (for example, the general experience level of the team members, prior experience working together) and the size of your development project (for example, larger projects may need more frequent reviews to ensure consistency across the project), you might choose to establish a validation checkpoint when each pair of domain–technical experts has reached what they consider to be a stable point with their portion of the analysis model, or you might choose to defer this level of review until after the design work associated with this portion of the model has been completed. If you choose the latter stage for your formal checkpoint (as we did for the IBM SanFrancisco frameworks), make sure that your teams have enough informal interaction with team leaders during the modeling process that potential side effects on other aspects of the model can be discovered and that design consistency across the framework can be maintained.

Solution

- Involve domain experts in developing the initial framework analysis model.
  - Preferably, at least one member of the domain team should have modeling experience.
  - Involve a developer with strong modeling skills to serve as a mentor to the domain team.
  - Don't assume that because a domain expert has data modeling experience that he or she will be an effective analysis modeler. Data modeling techniques are often at odds with good object modeling objectives.
- Use the initial analysis model as a basis for educating the technical team about the domain.
  - Begin the education process with high-level model walk-throughs led by domain experts.
  - Mix the approaches used during the follow-up education process: some developers prefer self-study with follow-up questions, while others prefer to be guided through the model.
- After the initial education process, encourage designers to work one-on-one with domain experts to complete the analysis model.
  - Pairing team members builds strong working relationships, further educates the technical member of the team in the domain details he or she needs to know, and allows the technical member to incorporate elements that will align the model with design objectives.
  - While not a primary goal, these sessions also allow designers to begin teaching domain experts about basic object-oriented design principles.

- Establish one or more checkpoints to validate the resulting model.
  - Ensure the model is consistent with other portions of the framework.
  - Check the level of information transfer between domain and technical members of the team.

When to Use/Not Use

Some form of knowledge transfer between domain and technical members of a development team on any software project is essential, and the earlier this transfer occurs within the natural development process, the better. This information transfer does not happen to the extent necessary of its own accord—you need to actively encourage it to occur. We've described various techniques that improve the likelihood of effective information transfer. Depending on the size and composition of your team, some or all of these techniques may be appropriate.

Applicability

- Whenever knowledge must be transferred between people with different levels of expertise, training, or skills, consider using the techniques described in this pattern. This includes not only domain knowledge transfer to technical developers but also transfer of software knowledge from the development team to the test team as well as other situations.

Known Uses

This pattern of communication has been used to improve the effectiveness of many software development projects. We used all of the techniques described in this chapter when developing the IBM SanFrancisco frameworks. In particular, we found that having the domain experts build the initial model served as a very useful point of communication since it gave the experts opportunities to explain their requirements to technical developers in a concrete manner. Coupled with one-on-one sessions to refine the analysis models, this proved to be the most efficient approach to reaching a complete and accurate analysis model.

Related Patterns

- Alles in Ordnung (Section 3.1)—transition of the analysis model to the design team is one of the key checkpoints in a framework development process.

- Innocent Questions (Section 3.2)—domain experts should ask innocent questions as part of design validation to ensure domain concepts are sufficiently covered by the design.

- Something Is Better Than Nothing (Section 5.2)—a strong analysis modeler from the technical team should participate with the domain team during initial analysis modeling.

- There Is No "I" in Team (Section 8.1)—use the techniques described by this pattern to help teams improve their communication.

- The Great Communicator (Section 8.2)—technical developers can gain a great deal of domain knowledge by participating in the initial analysis modeling and mentoring process.

Chapter

6

Design

The design process transforms analysis and requirements information into the true blueprints of your framework: framework elements defined within the constraints and capabilities of your target technology. This is where the framework's implementable classes, methods, and relationships are defined that, in total, work together to fulfill the behavior described in the use cases. Patterns that will assist you in the design phase include

- Pass the Buck (Section 6.1)—accepting that a framework can't and shouldn't make all the decisions for applications built by using it
- Missed It by That Much (Section 6.2)—using and iteratively creating patterns
- That's the Way the Cookie Crumbles (Section 6.3)—realizing that some patterns can be partially "prebuilt" as mini-frameworks
- It's Still OO to Me (Section 6.4)—recognizing that working on an object-oriented (OO) framework doesn't suddenly give you an exemption from good OO practices and that fixing bad OO practices is more difficult and potentially embarrassing with frameworks than with software

In this chapter we describe these patterns.

6.1 Pass the Buck

Also Known As

Knowing When a Framework Shouldn't Do Something

Intent

Most software development involves creating software that deals with every situation. Every contingency is mentioned, examined, and handled. Frameworks require that in some cases a contingency is mentioned, examined, and *not* handled.

Context

When you have a house built, you have a number of choices to make. Although you could work with an architect to make every single decision, most people pick a prearchitected house plan, which is similar to picking a framework. This gives you the core architecture for the house. You then work with the builder to decide how to complete the house. When you choose the prearchitected plan, you don't want to have to worry about every detail, such as which size nails or electrical wires are used. (These are specified by the building code and you'd only override them if you had a special case of some kind.) Instead you can concentrate on a list of normal extension points— things such as lights, colors, trim, and cabinets. Because of people's tastes, these are things that vary dramatically from house to house. Consider for a moment how you would react to a prearchitected plan that specified special plugs in all the ceilings that limited the lighting choices to three colors (pick three you hate). Now, to keep the colors in the house consistent, you have to pick wall colors that go with the awful color you were forced to pick, and you then need trim and cabinets that match. Would you be happy that the plan made this choice for you? That choice made it easier for you when you would have picked one of those lights anyway. However, since most people wouldn't—the colors were that bad—it would have been better if the plan hadn't specified the plugs in the first place.

Returning to the "real" world of software development, most developers have learned, quite correctly, that to develop bug-free and stable software they have to think about and handle all of the contingencies. We've all done this to varying degrees, the most extreme cases being low-level system code, such as operating system code. In operating system code, forgetting about a situation can have catastrophic results. A framework is different. Some decisions in a framework shouldn't be made. These are decisions that lock framework users into a particular solution when they actually need the flexibility of choosing from a number of solutions. For example, you should consider carefully where the framework would work with transactions. If the framework starts and commits transactions on its own, it becomes difficult for framework users to combine two methods that handle their own transactions into a single transaction—especially if the underlying infrastructure doesn't support nested transactions.

How do you make the right decision to completely defer some decisions while completely making others?

Example

Suppose that we designed the repair aspects of the clothing framework to always identify any clothing with tears, no matter how small, as needing repair. And further, suppose that the framework prevented any clothing flagged as needing repair from being selected for wear. Some users would be quite happy with this arrangement; however, others would find this approach too restrictive. In some circles, ripped clothing is the height of style, and even when this isn't the case, there are times and places when a shirt with a small tear is quite acceptable. By making what seemed to be a reasonable decision about repair algorithms, we've made it hard for many users to get the most out of our framework.

Problem

A framework has to balance between making and deferring decisions. Decisions can be completely made, partially deferred by using extension points, or fully deferred by not including any solution in the framework.

Approaches

The key to solving this problem is realizing that there are choices in how a framework supports multiple applications. Getting stuck in the belief that a framework has to solve all application problems prevents creation of a successful framework. You have to realize that there are decisions you can completely make, can partially make, and must fully defer, and you need to know which are which.

Decisions that are completely made are those things that are always done the same way by all applications. These are often things that end up in class libraries or common business objects. For example, every banking application needs to manage currencies and exchange rates, so objects for working with these can be provided. These are the easiest situations because you get to do it all.

Decisions that can be partially made are typically encountered when part of a process is variable. For example, in the exchange rate example above, while much of the support is fixed, the retrieval of an exchange rate can vary. A direct exchange rate can be required (U.S. dollars to Canadian dollars), inverses can be allowed (using one over Canadian dollars to U.S. dollars), and transitive exchange rates can be allowed (first using U.S. dollars to Euros, then Euros to Canadian dollars). Framework users must be able to make this decision. In these cases you have to work with your domain experts to determine that an extension point is needed and how it should be supported. These situations occur quite often when developing frameworks.

Fully deferred decisions are ones that you just shouldn't make. Making these decisions forces framework users to make other decisions in a way they don't want to make them. For example, in the currency exchange example, if we decide to update an exchange rate usage count each time a rate is used (read-only), we might decide to update this count within a transaction. If we make this decision, framework users will have to deal with lots of write-lock contention on the exchange rates. If nested transactions aren't supported, they will have to either modify the framework code or completely replace it. Since this is a Tor's second cousin situation—most people won't want this support—we really shouldn't make this decision in the framework. When these situations occur it is crucial that they are correctly identified.

As you can see from this example, these decisions can't be made in isolation. Areas of the framework, like the exchange rate support, may involve all three types of decisions at the same time. It is important to keep this in mind so that each situation is treated independently and not accidentally lumped together. For example, when we realize we can't add the transactions, we should not use this information to decide not to provide any exchange rate support—the decision impacts only the function that required the transaction.

Once you've accepted that the framework has these situations, how do you determine which type you're dealing with? We've found that the best approach is to start with the assumption that you'll be able to completely make the decision. The key is to make sure you don't get trapped there. Many of the other chapters in this book describe patterns for making sure you correctly identify and handle the cases where decisions should be partially deferred. The common thread throughout all of these patterns is to work with (and listen to) the domain experts to identify those places where variability is needed (as discussed in the Innocent Questions pattern, Section 3.2), making sure you don't overdo it (as described in the Tor's Second Cousin pattern, Section 4.2).

Even though you will typically assume that design decisions can be completely made within your framework, you need to keep an open mind (in other words, be skeptical). As you work with the domain experts you'll identify areas where variability is needed (using techniques in other chapters) and eventually try to figure out how to support that variability. This is the critical place to remember that you may want to completely defer the decision. Often these situations manifest themselves as cases where it becomes difficult to identify how or where the framework will support the variability. In other cases variability expands until it encompasses the entire process. For example, these processes become replaceable commands [Gamma 94] running over the framework business objects. These are cases where complete deferral should be considered. This approach can also be used to decide where the framework should stop. For example, you might encounter a process on which, beyond the fact that there is a process, domain experts cannot agree. This is a candidate for omission from the framework.

Another thing to keep in mind is how the decision restricts what framework users can do. In our transaction example, consider what it means when we make the decision about updating the exchange rate usage count—especially what it means to someone trying to use the framework. If, as in our transaction example and our clothing repair example above, a design decision traps users into an unacceptable situation, this is probably a case for going to either a partially made decision or a completely deferred decision. You probably won't get this right the first time, but you will discover these cases as your testing teams try to use the framework. As you look at the problems they discover, keep in mind that it may be a situation where the framework developers programmed a complete decision they shouldn't have.

Even if you decide not to do something, you should carefully consider documenting the decision as part of the framework. This documentation may be in the form of text describing why you decided not to do it or, more often, it will be in the form of examples of how it could be done. This is most important for items that will be added by a large number of customers. It shows that you thought about the situations and, even if the example doesn't exactly match their situation, it gives them a starting point for addressing their requirements.

Solution

- Realize that framework decisions come in three flavors:
    1. Completely covered—functions that the framework just does. Every application will do them this way.

2. Partially covered—functions that the framework provides as extension points. The portion that every application performs differently can be identified and encapsulated in some manner.

3. Fully deferred—decisions that the framework developers should not make. If made, these decisions would have ramifications that would force applications to do things a certain way when usually users will want to do it differently.

- During development:
  - Assume framework functions will be completely covered.
  - Be skeptical and use the techniques described in other chapters of this book to identify those functions that should be partially covered.
  - Recognize you may have a decision to fully defer when:
    - It is hard to determine where and how to support functional variability.
    - The variability grows to encompass the entire process.
  - Be aware of the ramifications of your decisions.
  - Be receptive to feedback from testing teams and be prepared to iterate.
  - Consider documenting fully deferred decisions—possibly with examples.

When to Use/Not Use

When developing a framework it makes sense to fully defer some decisions; however, for most other software development it does not. For example, application developers cannot fully defer any decisions. On the other hand, application developers want to conceptually cover some decisions only partially, that is, they want to add support for functional variability but also provide one or more complete implementations that support the variability. For example, if the Strategy design pattern [Gamma 94] were used for some function within an application, that application would provide specific strategies from which application users could choose—perhaps configuration through properties or parameterization.

Fully deferred decisions do occur in other reusable software. For example, a class library would be very likely to fully defer the handling of transactions.

Sometimes a decision may appear to be one that should be fully deferred because there are distinct solutions. However, when the solution space is small enough, you should consider providing all the solutions with the framework. For example, determining the cost for a product is normally done in one of five distinct ways. The method used in a particular situation is determined by legal and business requirements. The framework developer cannot decide which of the five a user is going to use. However, in this situation the framework can provide not only the five algorithms but also the other support needed in the framework. For example, if you use a fixed cost, you simply record the cost. If you use last-in, first-out costing (using the cost of the last item you bought), the framework can provide support for also keeping and managing all of the costs.

Applicability

- Application developers rarely, if ever, fully defer decisions, partially defer decisions via properties or parameterization, and completely cover most decisions.

- Developers of reusable software have situations in which decisions are fully deferred.

- If there are only a few solutions, framework developers should consider providing them all.

Known Uses

Completely and partially covered decisions have occurred in all software we've developed. Sometimes the number of partially covered decisions is very small. Fully deferred decisions were a new concept we encountered while working on the IBM SanFrancisco project.

Transactions were one area where the IBM SanFrancisco frameworks usually deferred the decision fully. In a few cases we were able to mark the transaction as rollback only. For example, when an exception occurred during object deletion we were unable to ensure everything deleted would be restored, so we marked the transaction as rollback only to ensure everything would be properly restored. In most cases we had to settle for documenting each method. This documentation gave framework users enough information to add transactions around the methods they wanted to combine into a single transaction.

Tax support was another area where the IBM SanFrancisco project fully deferred the decision completely. After discussion with the domain experts we determined that tax support varied so dramatically we would not be able to identify a common core we could provide.

Related Patterns

- Innocent Questions (Section 3.2)—make sure the decision being deferred is understood.

- Tor's Second Cousin (Section 4.2)—determine whether the decision should be deferred.

6.2 Missed It by That Much[1]

Also Known As

Developing and Applying Patterns

Intent

Patterns are key to developing a successful framework. They encourage consistency, create a new higher-level language, and increase the speed of development. Pattern development involves iteration. Using patterns, especially patterns you develop, requires caution.

Context

Patterns capture the essence of a solution to a problem in a manner that allows the solution to be applied to other problems in the same family. In other words, a pattern captures the core of how to solve a specific problem and the thinking behind that solution. This detail allows you to share the knowledge of those who've solved the problem before you and apply it to your problem. When applied to design, this not only creates a reusable design but also captures the tradeoffs inherent in that design. Patterns, however, cannot be applied blindly—just because a pattern provides a solution does not mean it is the right solution. In fact, even experienced object-oriented designers can become so attached to a particular pattern (or patterns) that they want to apply them everywhere—the "when you have a hammer, the whole world looks like a nail" syndrome. Experienced architects and team leaders need to put the brakes on this sort of thinking through another form of the What, Not How pattern (see Section 4.3), this time applied to designers instead of domain experts.

A framework is an ideal place to use patterns. A framework must have a way to allow itself to be extended. These *extension points* (often called *hotspots*) must be provided in a way that the framework consumer can quickly understand and leverage and that fulfills the extension requirements while preserving the overall integrity of the framework (for example, by preserving proper

---

1. Maxwell Smart is a bumbling spy character from the 1960s U.S. television comedy *Get Smart*. "Missed it by *that* much . . ." was his catch phrase after discovering an error in judgment or execution. Today's equivalent phrase (as blessed by the *Oxford English Dictionary*) is Homer Simpson's "Doh!"

encapsulation and isolation characteristics between framework classes and categories). We have observed that these extension points are not completely unique but can be grouped together into different kinds of extension points. Patterns are an ideal way to capture these extension mechanisms. This approach allows framework designers to keep consistency across the extension points and to create a language that both domain and technical experts can use for discussing the requirements of a specific extension point.

While working on the IBM SanFrancisco project, we found that many domain experts became conversant in design patterns to the point that they could meaningfully contribute to design discussions with technical developers. While not all domain experts reach this level of understanding patterns, you will find those who do become a huge asset to your development team—in effect, they become "great communicators" (as described in The Great Communicator pattern, Section 8.2) in their own right, smoothing the flow of information through the development team.

Using patterns in the framework meant we had to apply and extend existing patterns, create our own patterns, refine our patterns, and apply our own patterns. Through this process, we experienced many Maxwell Smart moments, "missing it by *that* much." We found that this iterative process was both a blessing and a curse. Our recommendation would be to always try to work with existing patterns first and to define your own pattern only when the existing patterns just don't fit.

Example

The simplest example of using an existing pattern for extension points is the use of the Strategy design pattern from the *Design Patterns* book [Gamma 94]. This pattern encapsulates an algorithm into a separate object. This separation allows the algorithm to vary independently of the object supporting the method.

Figure 6.1 demonstrates the Strategy pattern. The BusinessObject class supports a method businessMethod(); instead of hard-coding the implementation for this method on the BusinessObject class, the processing is deferred to another class. In this case it must be an instance of a class, such as Algorithm 1, that realizes the BusinessMethodStrategy interface. The algorithm used for BusinessObject's businessMethod() can be changed simply by creating a new realization or picking from one of the existing realizations of the Business-MethodStrategy interface.

In our clothing example, this is the ideal way to handle some of the differing requirements. Rather than trying to create an object that can support all the requirements, we need to identify processes or portions of processes that can

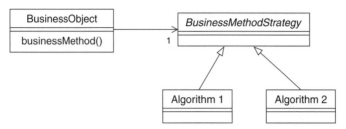

Figure 6.1 *The Strategy design pattern*

be pulled out into separate objects. You have to remember the Tor's Second Cousin pattern (see Section 4.2), since it is easy to think that every process (and method) needs to be modified by someone. Although the Strategy pattern could be used for each method, this quickly becomes unmanageable. Applying the principles of the Tor's Second Cousin pattern allows you to focus on only those processes (methods) that most people will need to modify.

In our clothing example, there are many places where the extension requirements can be fulfilled using the Strategy design pattern. In most cases, when selecting clothing the customer will want to be able to customize the selection to his or her particular needs. For example, the clown's selection algorithm is very likely to be completely different from the cowboy's. It is tempting to say that the selection algorithm is the same for wearing and the other processes (such as repair); however, while some aspects of this are true, these selection algorithms may be very different. In fact they may be very personal. For example, Squeaky-Clean the Clown probably wants a different algorithm for selecting what to clean than Yucko the Clown. If the algorithms are similar, they can utilize common functionality to realize their algorithms. This could be done using the Template Method design pattern [Gamma 94], which often goes hand in hand with the Strategy design pattern. The basic algorithm is implemented as a template method within a strategy base class, and specific strategy classes implement the various primitive operations of the template method as needed.

If, as described above, we can find an existing pattern, we have to ensure only that we apply it properly. What do we do if the pattern isn't quite right? What do we do if it doesn't match at all?

Problem

How do you know when to create a pattern rather than use an existing one? If needed, how do you create a new pattern?

Approaches

Rather than discussing our recommendations as independent items, we're going to look at the development of one of the IBM SanFrancisco patterns as a case study, then derive our recommendations from that case study. The pattern, called Chain of Responsibility Driven Strategy [Carey 00, p. 75], is a variation on the Strategy pattern.

While working on replenishment processing[2] in warehouse management, we discovered (by working with our domain experts) that we needed some way to vary the algorithm. Our first approach was to apply the Strategy design pattern, as shown in Figure 6.2. We have a recommendReplenishment() method on the Product, supported by a recommendReplenishmentStrategy strategy class with the same method.

In this case it appears that we were able to fulfill the extension requirements with the strategy. However, as we worked with the domain experts we discovered that having a unique algorithm for an individual product was not always the case. Sometimes the default replenishment algorithm varied based on the Warehouse and sometimes based on the Company managing the Warehouse. A complex strategy for our replenishment algorithm, one that would take into account the Warehouse and Product, could solve this.

We wondered if this was the only situation we would encounter like this on the project. Should we create a formal variation of the pattern—a new pattern—or should we simply keep this as a unique instance of the pattern? There are a couple of ways to determine this. One is to wait. Solve this problem now and then go on developing the framework. If you encounter the same (or similar) situation later, then come back and see if there is a pattern. This is often how we approached this. However, in this case our domain experts told us that this was something that would occur over and over. This

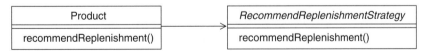

Figure 6.2   *Solving replenishment by using the Strategy design pattern*

---

2. Replenishment deals with what to do when you need more of something. This processing may be triggered when you run out of stock or when you fall below a certain level. In our example, we don't care why the replenishment process is being run (this is probably in an extension point supported by the Strategy design pattern); instead we are focused on the decision of how many more of the item we need to obtain, if any.

told us it was worth the time to investigate the creation of additional guidelines to the Strategy pattern or, if the variations warranted it, a new pattern.

The first thing we realized when we looked at these additional requirements for the extension point was that they were similar in concept to the Chain of Responsibility design pattern from the *Design Patterns* book [Gamma 94]. We wanted to find the first participant who could provide an algorithm. In our case, we first determined whether there was an algorithm defined for the Product, then the Warehouse, and finally the Company. We would use the first algorithm we found. Thus, as shown in Figure 6.3, we separated the original strategy into two classes, a selection strategy that encapsulated the chain of responsibility and traversed it searching for the second class, the replenishment algorithm.

This took a single, very complex strategy and decomposed it into a number of simpler strategies that could be mixed and matched. In fact, we could now define subclasses of the replenishment strategy and, by putting them on the appropriate participant in the chain or responsibility, have our selection strategy pick the correct algorithm, as shown in Figure 6.4.

For example, if we were managing an office supply warehouse, we might manage the products: pencils, pens, copiers, and file folders. We could also have two types of warehouses. One represents the supply cabinet where employees can retrieve whatever they need. The other type of warehouse is the central warehouse. We need to carefully mange the quantities of items being kept in

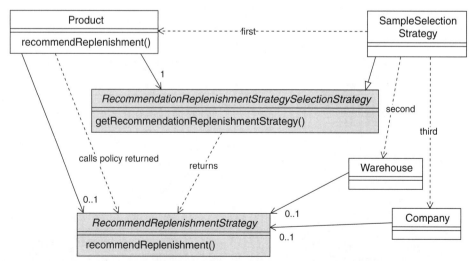

Figure 6.3   *Solving replenishment by using the Strategy design pattern twice*

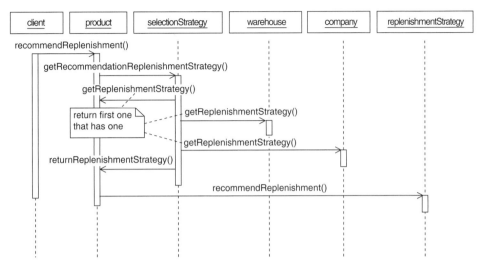

Figure 6.4   *Finding the replenishment strategy*

the warehouses. If we have too much, then we have a lot of money tied up in inventory that isn't being used. If we have too little, we either can't fulfill our orders or our employees can't do their jobs because they don't have what they need in the supply cabinet. As you can guess, this is an area where companies pay a great deal of attention and need the ability to adapt as business changes.

In the office supply example, the company's overall policy for replenishment is to always obtain 1,000 more when we run out (quantity = 0). Our central warehouse (used for restocking the supply cabinets) can use this policy. However, the supply cabinets can't hold 1,000 of each item, and it impacts productivity if employees have to wait for the pencils to run out before we replenish them. Thus this warehouse's policy is changed to always obtain 20 of each when the quantity reaches 5 or less. Also, copiers are very expensive and take up a lot of warehouse space, so no matter what, we never what to obtain more than one additional copier at any one time. Figure 6.5 shows these policies.

Now when we go to replenish a product, our selection algorithm will first look at the Product, then the Warehouse, and then the Company. The configuration shown in Figure 6.5 fulfills our requirements.

We made the next change to the candidate pattern when we realized that the selection algorithm could not be fixed to work only with a predefined set of participants. In other words, there would be cases when new participants, for example, ProductGroup, would need to be used by the selection strategy. This could be done with the candidate pattern but would require coordinated

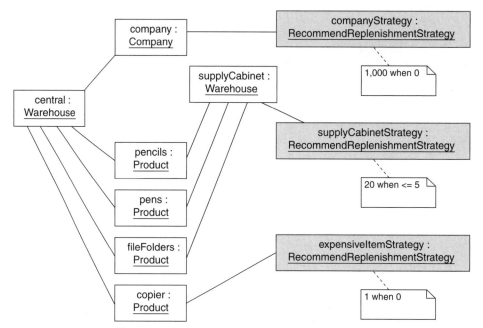

Figure 6.5   *Replenishment example with three strategies*

changes to add an attribute to every participant. We realized that we could use the Property Container pattern [Carey 00], which allows arbitrary attributes to be added by token, to add the strategies to whatever participants the selection policy used. The IBM SanFrancisco project provided most business objects so that they supported the Property Container pattern, thus allowing most business objects to be used by the selection policy without having to change their interface. The selection policy, rather than calling a specific method (getReplenishmentStrategy() in Figure 6.4), can simply call the getPropertyBy() method, passing a predefined token.

This candidate pattern now provides the needed flexibility to support any participants in the selection process and a straightforward family of replenishment algorithms that can be configured across these participants to extend the framework to meet a particular warehouse application's needs.

At this point, if we hadn't known we should start with a pattern, we'd need to go back to the situation (or situations) where we encountered the problem before and rework them to follow the new pattern. This should not be considered an optional step. It has two benefits: (1) it ensures consistency throughout the framework and (2) these additional uses help validate the pattern.

You probably noticed that we called this pattern a candidate pattern. Why? We have a pattern that fulfills our needs, so aren't we done with our pattern-defining work? The answer is "no"—until a pattern has been used at least three times in reasonably unique situations it should not be considered completed. Even then, you will still find improvements to the pattern. Each of these will need to be evaluated to determine whether they can or should be retrofitted back into any existing applications of the pattern.

In our case, the second real application of the pattern led us to an interesting additional requirement: that most of the time the selection strategy would find the replenishment strategy directly on the Product. In other words, most of the time we could skip the selection policy and go directly to the replenishment strategy on the Product. This put our pattern into a situation where the Tor's Second Cousin pattern could be applied—the selection strategy was not needed for most of our users and it added complexity and overhead to the normal case. This caused us to readdress the pattern to see if there were some way to incorporate this new requirement.

There are a number of possible outcomes to this dilemma. We might determine that the pattern just doesn't make sense in this situation. Do not try to force the requirements into the pattern. The pattern should fit nicely to the requirements. Often developers new to patterns become enamored with patterns and see patterns everywhere. This is best tempered by having someone with pattern experience as a team leader or pattern guardian (see the Consistency Czar pattern, Section 8.3). If it doesn't make sense, honestly ask if there is another existing pattern that should be used or if there might even be a new pattern—going back to the new pattern questions. In some cases, you'll discover that you can modify the pattern to include the new requirements. In any case, ensure you capture the thinking in the documentation for the patterns you consider. This knowledge of why the pattern did and, more importantly, didn't work for a particular case is invaluable to those who later try to determine if the pattern is one they should use for their problem.

In our case, we had an inspiration. The first part of this inspiration was that the selection strategy could, instead of returning the replenishment strategy, run the replenishment strategy and return the result. This meant that the method getRecommendationReplenishmentStrategy() on the selection strategy was replaced with a recommendReplenishment() method that not only retrieved the correct strategy to run but also ran it and returned its results. The second part was the realization that a replenishment strategy was in fact a selection strategy that selected itself. Thus, we can combine our two strategy hierarchies as shown in Figure 6.6.

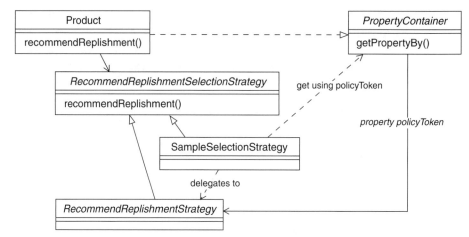

Figure 6.6   *Solving replenishment by using combined strategy heirarchies*

Combining the hierarchies now meant that in those cases where a selection wasn't needed, we could simply put the replenishment strategy in its place. This change eliminated the extra overhead of the selection strategy in our normal case. As we looked at this change, we decided it was worth reworking all uses of the pattern, since even in those cases where this requirement was not stated, it provided extra extensibility that our domain experts felt could be useful.

Another aspect that comes into play for pattern iteration is code generation. Often if you have code-generator support for patterns, changes to the patterns will be much easier to retrofit into existing implementations than those patterns that use hand-coded support. Also, as discussed in the That's the Way the Cookie Crumbles pattern (see Section 6.3), it is sometimes possible to provide a reusable implementation of a core portion of the pattern. This helps to encapsulate most changes to the core of the pattern so that they have little or no impact on the patterns using it.

Code generation also impacted what we decided to define as patterns. When something was completely generated, we were less likely to define it as a pattern. Instead the knowledge was captured in the code-generator rules and supporting programming model.

Solution

- Try to use existing patterns.
  - Don't force-fit them.
    - Sometimes they just won't match.
    - Sometimes there won't be a pattern.

- – Add documentation to them that is unique to your project or product.
- – Sometimes patterns can be combined.
- Identify new patterns if necessary.
  - – Don't rush defining the pattern.
    - Wait until the second or even third use.
    - Leverage domain experts to determine frequency.
    - Like existing patterns, don't force-fit them.
  - – Have a patterns guru (or architect).
    - Look for patterns across products.
    - Capture and enforce patterns.
  - – Iteration is part of using patterns you define. Refine over time—expect to iterate.
    - Changes typically are largest with the first few uses.
    - Be prepared to change existing uses to use updated patterns.
- Code generation can help with pattern usage.
- Be aware that patterns may be partially implemented.

When to Use/Not Use

There are a number of situations to watch out for when using existing patterns or creating and using your own patterns.

When learning about existing patterns, be careful not to think you have to "swallow the elephant." There are lots of patterns available (see *The Patterns Almanac 2000* [Rising 00]). If you try to learn them all, you won't get any development done. Learn at least a core few—we recommend at least those in the *Design Patterns* book [Gamma 94]—and then possibly some related to the area your application covers. Realize that this is knowledge that can grow over time. You can learn core patterns now and apply them and then learn new ones and apply them on your next project.

When applying a pattern, watch out for "hammer and nail" syndrome. In this syndrome, because you have a hammer, everything looks just like a nail. Too often with developers new to patterns, everything becomes a pattern, and suddenly patterns are used incorrectly or inappropriately. While we do believe patterns are everywhere, we just don't believe that every line of code we write must conform to one or more patterns.

When defining your own patterns, watch out for unnecessary complexity. It is important to have people review your pattern and push on it to refine it. In some cases your pattern may be quite complex. Our only suggestion is to push hard on that complexity to make sure it is there because it is really needed.

For example, one trap we've seen is adding a feature because it can be done, not because any domain person would ever conceive of using the function. Just because you could vary airline ticket prices by the second doesn't mean you should do so; allowing them to change every minute is sufficient.

Our experience with defining patterns is that a typical pattern in its formative stages goes through cycles of complexity. A pattern starts out relatively simple, then as additional requirements are added, it becomes more and more complex. At a certain point, it becomes clear that the complexity is outweighing the benefits of the pattern. Often we find that refactoring a pattern at this point is possible and very useful. Many of the patterns developed during the IBM SanFrancisco project went through two or three simple-to-complex-to-simple cycles before we were satisfied with them.

One thing that can help when defining patterns is to look at the meta-patterns (underlying principles) behind extension patterns in frameworks. This is discussed in *Design Patterns for Object-Oriented Software Development* [Pree 95].

Just because you've defined a pattern doesn't mean you have to document that pattern formally. Document to the level you need for your project. This may be no documentation, when you have a patterns guru who personally provides education and support. Documentation can always be formalized later. The one caveat, as discussed in the Souvenirs pattern (Section 7.1), is to capture enough information as you go along that you can write the formalized documentation when you need it.

Applicability

- Learn the existing patterns in stages.
    - First learn the core patterns in the *Design Patterns* book [Gamma 94].
    - Then learn patterns that apply to your application's domain.
    - Learn other patterns over time.
- Patterns are like any other tool and can be overused. Don't fall into the "hammer and nail" syndrome.
- Watch out for complexity in patterns you define. Push hard on the complexity, but don't be afraid to keep it when it is needed.
- Meta-patterns can help provide a foundation for defining your own patterns.
- Documentation can be written over time.
    - Keep at least enough information to properly document the pattern later.
    - Decide what to document, how much to write, and when to create the documentation based on your particular needs.

Known Uses

We used this pattern for each of the patterns used and developed for the IBM SanFrancisco project.

Related Patterns

- Tor's Second Cousin (Section 4.2)—determine the extensibility needed so the right pattern can be applied.
- What, Not How (Section 4.3)—if you let patterns drive your design, you may not be ensuring you are addressing requirements and not implementations.
- That's the Way the Cookie Crumbles (Section 6.3)—sometimes the core portion of a pattern can be implemented in a reusable manner.
- Souvenirs (Section 7.1)—even if at first you don't document a pattern formally, keep enough information so you can at some point in the future.
- The Great Communicator (Section 8.2)—a pattern-savvy domain expert can partially fill the role of the great communicator.
- Consistency Czar (Section 8.3)—this person can also guard against pattern misuse and abuse.

6.3 That's the Way the Cookie Crumbles

Also Known As

Patterns Can Be Mini-Frameworks

Intent

A pattern is usually only thought of as providing a recipe (that is, a cookie-cutter approach) for applying the design it captures to a particular problem. There are also situations where a core portion of the pattern can be provided as a mini-framework (or framelet). Although using the mini-framework is optional, it can provide a jump start when applying the pattern.

Context

We've found that patterns are a key ingredient to building a successful framework. Identifying and applying patterns is discussed in detail in the Missed It by That Much pattern (see Section 6.2). As we used and developed patterns within the context of a framework we discovered that in some patterns there is a common core—certain things are always done the same way (that is, generically) no matter to what problem you apply the pattern. We found that in this situation a mini-framework (or framelet [Pree 01]) can be provided that addresses this core. Each application of the pattern can then use this mini-framework to solve its unique problem.

Example

In the clothing selection portion of our framework, we need a way to write a selection algorithm that can work with highly variable criteria; there must be a way for users of the clothing framework to add (or remove) criteria when they develop their particular applications. For example, clown clothing selection might require the addition of clothing brightness and the removal of "good taste" criteria such as restricting certain patterns (like stripes and plaids) from being worn together. We have the same problem when it comes to repair. A clown may want to include special stain identification as part of the process—sending clothing stained by elephant dung to a cleaner that specializes in elephant stains. Without going into detail,[3] these are essentially the same problem—providing an algorithm so that it can work with varying criteria without being tied to the exact criteria. Using what we learned in the Missed It by That Much pattern, we can create a pattern for this (assuming we can't identify one that already solves this problem). Once we've identified a pattern, how do we determine whether it should be a normal pattern or a mini-framework pattern?

Problem

How do you identify, capture, and use mini-framework patterns?

Approaches

A valid approach is to not bother with mini-frameworks at all. Just as with any reuse technique, the end must justify the means. In other words, are you doing this only once? Or do you think you are going to do it only once? You can always change to use a mini-framework in a later iteration. In our example,

---

3. For a complete discussion of this pattern see the Key/Keyable pattern in the *SanFrancisco Design Patterns* book [Carey 00].

we could simply apply the pattern in both cases independently and every-thing would work out fine.

Why think about using a mini-framework at all? The advantages of using a mini-framework are the same as those for any reuse technique. You can take the mini-framework and know that the core of the solution will work (and the code implementing that core has already been extensively tested), you can focus on just what makes your use of the pattern unique, and, just like a pat-tern, you can take advantage of the knowledge already used to solve the problem.

So how do you know if you should identify a mini-framework pattern instead of a cookie-cutter pattern? First you have to realize that some patterns should not be supported by a mini-framework. For example, creating a mini-frame-work to support the Strategy design pattern [Gamma 94] doesn't provide any value and, in fact, increases the likelihood of coding errors using that pattern (because every method invocation involving a strategy will require a down-cast to be executed).

Adding a mini-framework normally requires the addition of new abstrac-tions. If the overhead of these abstractions is greater than their reuse value, then a mini-framework should not be created. Consider how the Adapter design pattern from *Design Patterns* [Gamma 94] is applied to two objects to allow them to work together. This pattern requires the adapter to understand the two objects it is adapting to one another. In most cases there are only two objects and this is done only once for the classes involved in the pattern, so a mini-framework would be of little value. However, if one object is often involved, we may be able to provide a mini-framework for adapting to that particular object. The Article object (see Figure 6.7) from the clothing frame-work will be used with a number of other applications. These applications don't work with Articles but expect different objects. We can provide adapters to make the Article object appear as the object they require. This is all we have to do.

If we try to build a mini-framework, we see that we can't do anything about the side of each adapter that deals with the other frameworks. Each adapter must be unique for each use of the Adapter pattern. On the Article side of the Adapter pattern, we may be able to provide a mini-framework. We could accomplish this by creating a class that adapts the Article to something from which it is easier to build the required adapters. This class, ArticleAdapter, would then be subclassed to provide specific adapters. Was this worth it? It depends. Does the ArticleAdapter class provide enough reuse to be worthwhile? It doesn't seem like it does in this case. In other cases it will be worthwhile.

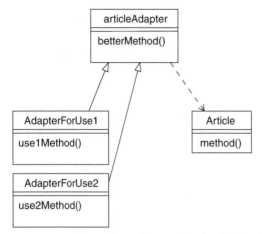

Figure 6.7   *Providing adapters for the Article class in the clothing framework*

A case in which it is worthwhile to identify and use a mini-framework is in the encapsulated criteria example. A new abstraction, Keyable, that encapsulates each individual criteria can be created. Keyable supports only equals but allows creation of Keyable subclasses that contain different criteria, such as a ColorKeyable. A set of criteria can then be encapsulated in another new abstraction, called a Key. The Key consists of Keyables and can support equals by delegating to each of the Keyables. For example, if the criteria are color and size, a Key composed of two Keyables that contain Red and 5, respectively, can be compared to a Key that contains Green and 5. The code using the Key class does not need to know what criteria is contained in the Key. Adding new criteria only requires that the creation of the Key be changed to add a new Keyable for new criteria.

A user of the Key mini-framework creates a usage-specific subclass (such as a SelectionKey), and this subclass exposes usage-specific methods (such as set-Color(), which creates the ColorKeyable containing the passed color and puts it into the Key). A family of Keyable subclasses that support a variety of things can also be provided. In this way the mini-framework provides a lot of reuse, allowing the Key pattern to be more rapidly applied.

When should we consider creating a mini-framework? Consider it if the core of the pattern can be identified and properly abstracted. In other words, can the algorithm defined by the pattern be partially or completely implemented by a class or classes that work solely with abstractions? If this is the case, a mini-framework might be worthwhile. If, on the other hand, specific details of the involved classes must be understood to implement the pattern's algorithm, a mini-framework is likely to not be a good choice and may in fact introduce a greater likelihood of development error.

Solution

- Not all patterns can be supported by mini-frameworks.
- Patterns whose algorithms can be partially or completely implemented through abstractions are candidates for a mini-framework.

When to Use/Not Use

It is easy to fall into the trap of thinking that the mini-framework is the pattern, for example, thinking that the Key and Keyable classes are the pattern. This misses the fact that the pattern is really the encapsulation of criteria so that algorithms can be independent of the criteria—allowing it to change. Losing sight of this can lead to confusion because there may be cases where the mini-framework is not applicable but the pattern is. For example, if we have all Boolean criteria (and will never have anything other than Booleans), it is probably better for performance reasons to implement the pattern using an array of Booleans, skipping the use of the Key and Keyables. If the Key and Keyable classes are the pattern, this isn't possible.

Don't force-fit a mini-framework. It doesn't make sense to support some patterns with a mini-framework. These cases, as described in the example above, bring more complexity with no value.

Make sure it is worth creating a mini-framework. As with any reuse technique, just because you can create a mini-framework doesn't mean it is helpful to create one. There isn't a specific rule for when it is worth doing; however, keep in mind how many times the mini-framework will be used and how much of the pattern can be provided. If it will be used only a few times and only a small portion of it can be provided, it probably isn't worth doing.

Don't forget you can always go back and add the use of the mini-framework. Since the mini-framework is not the pattern, going back and adding the use of a mini-framework to code already using the pattern does not change the pattern. Often, if there are not clear indications that this will be a common problem, it isn't worth the time to create the mini-framework. Just like patterns, mini-frameworks go through iterations, so it is worth waiting for more than one usage to reduce the iterations.

Applicability

- A mini-framework is not a pattern. A mini-framework is a way of implementing the use of a pattern by providing its core algorithm in an abstract form.
- Don't force-fit a mini-framework on a pattern.
- Don't create a mini-framework just because you can.
- Don't rush to create a mini-framework.

Known Uses

As part of developing the IBM SanFrancisco frameworks a number of mini-frameworks were identified. One example is the Key/Keyable pattern described in the Approaches section above. This pattern became the basis for a number of other patterns used in that project. Another mini-framework we found was the Extensible Item pattern [Carey 00]. This pattern allows an object to support dynamic changes in behavior and data, simulating dynamic inheritance. We used this as the basis for implementing a number of business objects that changed their behavior and data as they were processed—traversing a domain-specific life cycle.

Related Pattern

- Missed It by That Much (Section 6.2)—creating mini-frameworks is part of developing and applying patterns.

6.4 It's Still OO to Me

Also Known As

Frameworks Aren't Exempt from Good and Bad Object-Oriented Practices

Intent

Working on an object-oriented framework doesn't suddenly give you an exemption from all the good object-oriented practices you've learned on other development projects. In fact, with more of the framework exposed to the framework user (the customer), fixing bad object-oriented practices is more difficult and potentially embarrassing.

Context

You're probably asking yourself why this section is even here. Isn't this so obvious it makes us look stupid to have even thought of including it in this book? When we started developing frameworks, we'd have agreed with you. Having been there and forgotten the rules embodied in this pattern, we think it is worth a short section of warning—especially if it saves you the time (and rework) you'll experience if you succumb to this temptation.

You won't start off to use bad object-oriented practices. It may be that you'll have developers new to object-oriented development on the team, and as a team leader you'll be mentoring them in good object-oriented practices. They'll have good arguments for why they are doing what they are doing. Your "gut" will know it's bad, but they'll convince you—or you'll convince yourself—and into the framework it goes. Or it may be that the team members just don't have the object-oriented experience, so they make the mistakes that come with inexperience.

Another way to look at this is that you can develop a better framework by applying good object-oriented practices. For example, good abstractions make the framework more reusable and understandable, and bad inheritance should be avoided. A myriad of other object-oriented practices are covered in depth in other books [Cline 95, Meyers 97]. In fact, many of the situations that originally drove these object-oriented practices are commonplace in the framework environment. For example, when using the Strategy design pattern [Gamma 94] it is crucial to get the method on the strategy right. This method on the abstract base class must be able to support any possible concrete implementation.[4] This makes it crucial that the method name and parameters are a good abstraction of all of these possible implementations.

Example

In the clothing example, we realize that the selection of clothing for wearing, repairing, cleaning, and purchasing has many similar characteristics. As a result, we create a set of abstract base classes: a class that holds the selection of items, called the Selection class, and the class that it holds, called Selectable. Figure 6.8 shows these two classes. Then, so we can add behavior and attributes specific to working with what to wear, we inherit SelectionToWear from Selection and Wearable from Selectable, as shown in Figure 6.9. This

---

4. However, when considering the possibilities, don't forget about the Tor's Second Cousin pattern (see Section 4.2).

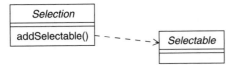

Figure 6.8   *Selection and Selectable classes in the clothing framework*

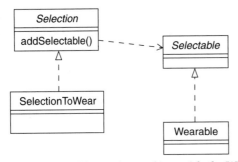

Figure 6.9   *Classes for working with the Wearable subclass*

looks great until you start looking at the methods that are inherited. This inheritance is breaking contravariance—requiring more or promising less. The method addSelectable(), which SelectionToWear inherited from Selection, takes a Selectable as a parameter. However, when SelectionToWear provides an implementation of the addSelectable() method it requires more; a Selectable is not enough since the parameter must implement the Wearable interface. The contract of the method indicates that any class that implements the Selectable interface is acceptable, however, the implementation requires a specific subclass (Wearable). In other words, SelectionToWear implementation of the method requires more than its base class's contract for the method—breaking contravariance.

Are you saying "It breaks contravariance, so what?"[5] We don't blame you if you are. In most cases breaking contravariance is a bad idea, but it usually isn't catastrophic. It becomes catastrophic in a framework because of the exposure a framework has. If you were building an application around the SelectionToWear class, the user interface wouldn't expose the contract of the

5. If you are saying "So what," you're probably basing this on what we call "consistent breakage of contravariance." In some cases there is no intent to ever use the abstraction (inheritance for code reuse in this case). Even though the subclass breaks contravariance, we know it will never encounter anything less that the "more" it requires. We also know that although it promises less, we will never expect more (that is, what the base class promises).

inherited methods; the user interface won't mention the fact that you're actually working with Selectables. On the other hand, when using a framework, customers are faced with dealing with these methods. They have to understand why inheritance is being used and how to work with these methods. In addition, they'll start wondering why the abstraction is there and how all the different things that inherit from it are related. In other words, they'll look for a use of the abstraction and when they can't find it, they won't believe there truly isn't any. They will believe that they simply haven't found it yet.

Problem

How do you ensure you'll keep using good object-oriented practices?

Approaches

The best approach is to have experienced object-oriented developers on the team. The best (and probably unrealistic) situation is to use developers who all have years of object-oriented experience. The realistic approach is to have a core group that can review designs and mentor less experienced developers. Members of this core group must be involved in the formal reviews (requirements handoff and combined review) in your development process (see the Alles in Ordnung pattern, Section 3.1), but that won't be enough. They should also be available before and after these reviews to help refine the framework designs. Usually it makes sense to make these experienced developers the team leaders and architects on the project.

Always keep in mind that these are best *practices* and sometimes they will need to be broken for valid reasons. This isn't to say you should encourage that, but you should be sensitive to what led the developer to a particular design. Usually this won't cause you to keep the design but will lead you to the right solution—perhaps through refactoring the existing design [Fowler 99], perhaps by applying another design pattern to the problem, or perhaps by working together to solve a truly novel design problem.

In the selection example above there are at least two solutions to explore: duplication of the code and reuse by containment. Duplicating the code eliminates potential confusion by fully separating the involved classes. This fixes the contravariance problem, but at the expense of code reuse. This may be appropriate if there are only a few (two) cases or if there is very little that doesn't need to be modified for each use.

Another solution is to take the function that was reused by inheritance and reuse it by containment instead. The Selection and Selectables classes become a mini-framework (see the That's the Way the Cookie Crumbles pattern, Section 6.3) that can be used by containment in each of the situations. This fixes our contravariance problem and preserves code reuse. The downside is that some of the methods that were inherited now require some programming, although many are simple wire-through methods.

Solution

- Build a core team of experienced object-oriented developers. Place these developers in leadership positions (architects and team leaders) throughout your development organization.
- Make sure those experienced developers are deeply involved in framework design.
  - They should participate in all key checkpoint reviews.
  - They should mentor less experienced developers throughout the design process.
- Don't condemn incorrect object-oriented practices. Understand the requirements that lead to them and use them to figure out the right solution—even if it turns out to be bad object-oriented programming.

When to Use/Not Use

Always be aware that these are best practices and there will be some unique situations where they don't apply. For example, the IBM SanFrancisco frameworks support a concept called class replacement [Carey 00]. Class replacement enhances the Class Factory pattern from the *Design Patterns* book [Gamma 94] to allow configuration to control which actual class is used when instantiating an object. In other words, the code creates and uses an object Foo, but it is created via a factory. We can reconfigure the factory so that instead of a Foo object, it returns anything that implements Foo's interface—instead of the original Foo object. From the discussion above you can see that this probably[6] breaks contravariance—especially when other classes are involved. Going back and looking at the requirements that drove class replacement as a solution, we see that the key requirement is the ability of framework users to define their own versions of a class created by the framework without having to locate and replace all of that creation code. The intent is not that there are multiple implementations of Foo in existence in any one

---

6. There are situations when you can adhere to the contract completely.

deployment of the framework. Instead, there will be one Foo implementation that is defined by the framework user. Although we may have broken contravariance in the design, when the code is running, there will only ever be one Foo implementation, and it will be aware of itself and the actual implementations of other classes it uses. This is a consistent breaking of contravariance—while we may promise less than the contract, we can guarantee that the contract is used only to the extent of the new promise.

Don't assume you should ignore an object-oriented practice. All other solutions should be explored first and, if it does end up being ignored, careful guidelines and documentation should be provided so that framework users can figure out what and why it is the way it is.

Applicability

- Sometimes object-oriented practices have to be ignored to solve a particular problem.
  - Do not do this lightly—try everything else first.
  - If you do this, provide lots of documentation.

Known Uses

We've applied (or at least tried to apply) best practices to all of our object-oriented development.

Related Patterns

- Alles in Ordnung (Section 3.1)—methodical development processes help ensure good object-oriented practices are followed.
- That's the Way the Cookie Crumbles (Section 6.3)—patterns can be used to promote good object-oriented practices.

Chapter

7

Documentation

One of the key differences when developing a framework versus any other software is the importance of documentation. With frameworks, the documentation is not just supporting the product but is actually a part of the product. As such, more consideration and care must be given to this topic, both when defining what documentation elements are important to your framework and when producing that documentation. Helpful patterns to consider when developing documentation include

- Souvenirs (Section 7.1)—deciding what core artifacts you will keep up-to-date so you can later create the full documentation (since it's likely you won't be able to keep all the documentation up-to-date and synchronized)
- Give 'Em What They Want (Section 7.2)—considering the framework's consumers when writing the documentation

These two patterns are discussed in this chapter.

7.1 Souvenirs

Also Known As

Keeping Just Enough to Write Documentation Later

Intent

Keeping documentation up-to-date is very difficult. An alternative to fully documenting everything as you develop the framework is to capture just enough information as you go along so you can use it to create the documentation later.

Context

When you travel, how do you remember the places you've visited? Everyone does it in different ways. Some people keep detailed diaries of their entire trip, while others rely completely on memory. Many people buy souvenirs at each of the major places they visit. These souvenirs help stimulate the memory by providing some information about the place visited. Usually when you travel you have limited luggage space for souvenirs, so you have to make sure you buy the best ones you can, the ones that will help you do the best job of remembering the details when you're telling your envious friends about your trip. For example, one of our friends collects beer glasses from around the world, but not just any beer glasses—they must be beer glasses from which he drank beer in a bar in another country. This certainly makes for some interesting stories.

Most software developers hate writing documentation. They rely completely on memory to remember what they did to develop the software. Documentation is usually the last thing they do, and they do it only if they can't get out of it. This, coupled with how critical documentation is for framework users, creates a potentially fatal situation for the project. If the framework is shipped without the documentation, it will be difficult (approaching impossible) to use. Not only is the documentation crucial but also there is need for lots of it. In fact, you may ship more documentation than code—at least it will feel like that! More documentation means more coordination of documents to keep them synchronized with one another, especially when iterating. For example, an error found during system testing may be identified as a code bug that to fix requires changing the contract of the method. The method is exposed in use cases and models, which must be reviewed to ensure that the contract change does not impact other use cases and model elements. And so on back up the chain. This ripple can go back and forth, with the worst case being an error that uncovers a requirements error, which in turn mandates a requirements change that ripples back out to the code. No matter what you do you'll encounter a few of these situations.

Example

The clothing framework ships with the following documents: domain guide, requirements, use cases, analysis models, design models, Javadoc, and sample guide. Because our framework has been partitioned into coarse-grained component categories, each of these categories has its own detailed documentation that must be coordinated and synchronized with other framework documentation. The full set of framework documents must all be up-to-date when the framework is shipped so that framework users can understand and extend the framework to do what they need to do.

Problem

How do you make sure you have up-to-date documentation when you ship the framework?

Approaches

There are many different approaches to ensuring that the documents are finished when the framework ships. The two extremes are: (1) keep the documentation up-to-date as development progresses or (2) write the documentation when you've completed development.

Keeping the documentation up-to-date as you go along ensures that the framework documents are ready to ship as soon as the code is ready to ship. There is no lag time when the documentation has to be written or cleaned up. The downside is that a lot of effort must be expended to keep the documentation up-to-date. Also, the nature of iteration (as discussed in the Iterate, Iterate, Iterate pattern, Section 3.5) is that the same things change a number of times. Thus, the same documentation will be reworked over and over again—which potentially frustrates developers as unnecessary work. Our observation is that when it comes to the code, these kinds of changes aren't a problem for developers, but with documentation rework, the complaints come pouring in.

Writing the documentation when you're all done with the code means that you have to plan for a delay between when you finish development and when you can ship the product—not the best story to have to play out in this day and age when rapid product delivery is essential. However, this is the least of our worries in this pattern—the more critical problem is the volatility of people's memories, especially when iteration is involved. Discussing multiple solutions in great detail tends to, over time, cloud memories of which one was accepted, especially when the final decision ends up being made arbitrarily. In addition, the reasons behind certain decisions tend to get lost. Why did we reject this alternative solution? Why did we pick this solution? The answers to these questions can make the documentation extremely useful, both for framework maintainers and framework users (see the Give 'Em What They Want pattern, Section 7.2). Another factor is that this knowledge is captured in a finite set of heads. If the people attached to these heads are no longer available, the information may be irrecoverable—even if the event that originally generated the knowledge is recreated.

Somewhere in between these two extremes is the right answer. The exact point is up to you, based on your particular project. We have found that it is important to retain and maintain certain key documents or portions of documents (our souvenirs), to synchronize documents at key points, and to use tooling to minimize the number of places that documentation is duplicated.

As long as a core set of documents is retained and maintained, the complete documentation can be quickly created at the end. In our clothing selection example, we might have the domain experts keep the requirements and use cases, leaving the creation of the domain guide until they are complete. For use cases, we could decide that only "interesting" use cases (that is, those that do something unique) will be written. If they simply set values or delete business objects, they aren't needed. (However, if they do any amount of domain logic, such as validation checking, they should be included in the documented set.) What has to be retained and maintained must be explicitly specified so everyone on the team knows. A place should also be defined where information (and ideas) for the other documents can be written down and kept for use when working on those documents.

Whether you maintain all the documents or only a core set, we have found it advantageous to ensure the documents that are kept are synchronized at key points. The key points work best if they are part of a methodical development process (see the Alles in Ordnung pattern, Section 3.1). In our clothing selection example, we would verify that the requirements and use cases matched at the requirements handoff and that the use cases and design match during the combined review. It is useful to have a final review in which someone from each team works with information development during the final cleanup to make sure that everything remains consistent.

One of the biggest synchronization problems occurs when the same information exists in two places. For example, the design model and the source code both contain documentation for the methods: in the design model they show up as descriptions and in the source code as Javadoc. The best solution is to pick one place to be the master for the information and, if possible, to generate the other from it. For the IBM SanFrancisco project, we used a code generator that took the design models and generated classes and skeletal code for us. In addition, it took the description in the design model and used it to generate the documentation in the code, which shows up as Javadoc. As tooling improves, this general approach will become much easier to do. Over time, we expect that tools supporting broader traceability will become more common,[1] for example, linking between different formats of information such as from the textual requirements to the graphical use cases and analysis model, from the graphical use cases to the textual use cases, and on to the design and source code for those use cases.

Solution

- Two extreme approaches exist for providing framework documentation.
  1. Defer documentation until the end of the project.
     - This causes minimal rework.
     - However, information gets forgotten.
     - You have to accept a large delay between code completion and product delivery.
  2. Keep the documentation up-to-date as you go along.
     - This creates lots of rework.
     - However, nothing gets forgotten.
     - You can deliver the product, including documentation, when code is complete.
- Instead of adopting one of these extremes, find a middle ground between the two approaches that is appropriate for your project.
  - Retain and maintain key documents (or portions of documents).
  - Synchronize documents at key points.
  - Minimize duplication via tooling.

When to Use/Not Use

We've found that the worst thing to rely on is people's memory, especially when people are transitory members of the team. When they leave, the information

---

1. See http://www.logiclibrary.com.

leaves with them. This is not a case of people being malevolent. We've found that the vast majority of the people with whom we've worked want the project to succeed. However, the realities of deadlines—the day those people leave—mean there is only so much information they can try to pass on . . . and it's only what they remember at that time.

For example, if you hire domain experts temporarily, when they're gone, the framework implementation becomes a substitute for missing framework requirements (a variation on the What, Not How pattern, Section 4.3). This substitution can be disastrous when transitioning the framework to other technologies or trying to fix bugs in the implementation. We are not implying that this loss of information occurs only with domain experts. This is equally a problem with the technical experts, since they can quickly forget why one design was chosen over another.

Be careful not to fall into the trap of shipping the core set of documentation as your final documentation. The logic that says, "It was good enough for creating the framework, so it must be good enough for using the framework," doesn't hold here. The differences in audience (see the Give 'Em What They Want pattern, Section 7.2) between framework producer and framework consumer are broad enough that information really needs to be tailored to the different framework users before it is shipped.

What you need to do depends on your particular project. If you have a small, quickly developed project, it may be appropriate to keep all the documentation up-to-date. If the framework developers are also going to be the framework users, it may be appropriate to forgo the documentation and add it as they use the framework.

Applicability

- It is dangerous to rely on people's memories for creation of documentation.
  - Human memory is very volatile.
  - People might leave and take knowledge with them.
- Lack of information can turn implementations into requirements.
- Partial development documentation should not be mistaken for complete documentation.
- Your project's specific characteristics can impact the solution.
  - For small projects, you may be able to keep all documentation up-to-date.
  - For internally consumed frameworks, you may be able to create documentation over time.

Known Uses

We've used this and similar techniques for a number of projects in less formal ways. In other words, we've kept a file drawer (both literally and figuratively) with the design sketches and notes in it and used it as the basis for complete documentation. When we did this for the IBM SanFrancisco project, we formally identified key documents (and portions of those documents) that needed to be retained and maintained, we synchronized the documentation as part of our process (see Appendix B), and we provided our own tooling to generate code from the design model to minimize duplication.

Related Patterns

- Alles in Ordnung (Section 3.1)—a methodical development process can help ensure that the correct items are kept to enable production of the documentation at the end of the project.

- Iterate, Iterate, Iterate (Section 3.5)—because you are likely to make multiple passes through your framework, leave enough information behind to allow you to recreate what you need later; don't try to write all you need the first time through.

- What, Not How (Section 4.3)—it's very easy for implementation to become a substitute for requirements if sufficient information is not kept.

- Give 'Em What They Want (Section 7.2)—the information you are keeping may be used to create documentation for a number of framework audiences.

7.2 Give 'Em What They Want

Also Known As

Different Framework Audiences Have Different Needs

Intent

Framework documentation has to target a specific audience. This means that some information may need to be duplicated into different documents in different forms for different audiences.

Context

How do you explain to your mother what you do for work? Is it the same way you explain it to someone you're hoping will hire you? Probably not. You have to evaluate the listeners and give 'em what they want. In other words, you have to explain it in terms they will understand and appreciate.

Developing and using a framework are two very different activities done by two different groups. Developing a framework involves looking at groups of requirements and providing a core solution to that group of requirements. Using a framework involves taking a specific set of requirements and determining how the framework can be used to fulfill these requirements—from both domain and technical perspectives. In one case (framework development), software that can be extended and reused is being developed. In the other (construction of a specific application), software that requires no flexibility, or at least a lot less,[2] is needed.

Thus, documentation aimed at these different groups, or audiences, has to be written specifically to them. This isn't a surprise to anyone who has written an article or a book, since knowing and addressing the target audience is crucial to success. For example, if you are building a framework, you need to build some extension point support into all classes of a certain type supplied with the framework. Since that support will apply to all of these classes, the documentation can be written with this rule or assumption. Thus, if the framework requires that all domain-level classes support the ability to dynamically add attributes, the documentation can simply state this as a rule.

On the other hand, when developing an application, the same level of flexibility is not needed, thus the same support may not need to be built into all classes of that type. Continuing with the above example, not every domain-level class in a specific application needs to support the addition of dynamic attributes. The framework developer had to do it to make sure the flexibility was available if needed, but the application developer knows whether or not it is needed and can decide not to provide the support. The documentation needs to reflect the fact that the application developer has to make a decision—rather than follow a rule.

---

2. For customizable applications you want to use similar extension capabilities but to a lesser and more controlled extent. Often framework extensions are externalized to application users as limited sets of selectable values (for example, controlling which algorithm is used as part of a function implemented via the Strategy design pattern). This can be thought of as the application developer taking the framework customized in a white-box manner and presenting the application as a black-box customization.

One tempting solution is to provide the documentation only for the application developer. However, this approach is inadequate. The application developer typically needs the framework developer's programming guide in order to understand what the framework is doing and why. In addition, some customers will see the benefit of frameworks and will want to create their own. The framework developer's programming guide will be invaluable to them. This also helps your framework because it adds another framework to the family of frameworks using the same standards—validating them for you and for the framework-consuming community.

In addition to the two technical audiences described above, there is also a domain audience. This domain audience needs to understand what the framework can do from a domain perspective. Domain experts don't care that we've used some really cool design approaches (such as the Strategy design pattern [Gamma 94]) in the framework—they want to know whether they can easily specify the business algorithm to be whatever they want. They also want to read about this in their terms. The framework, by the very nature of having abstractions, has a number of things that domain experts may not recognize. A common reason for this is that the framework supports building applications in different countries that have different ways of doing things. The framework has to pick one name, so somebody's name has to win—and this name will be recognized only by the domain experts from that country. An alternative is to pick a new name that isn't used by anyone, but this just means everyone is equally confused. Having tried this, we don't recommend it. Instead we recommend picking the term used in the main demographic or the most common term.

Example

When developing the clothing selection portion of the framework, we need to support its use by clowns, cowboys, and other people. Each of these users has a unique perspective of clothing and the extensibility needed in the different parts of the framework. We've created user guides and requirements documents, but these are about what the framework provides in terms used by the framework. They show all the possible extension points that could be used. They have no concept of what is appropriate for each of the individual domains. Also, we documented our programming guide, which is oriented toward helping the framework developer create the best possible framework. We're about to ship the framework to the customers with all this great documentation. Will they be able to do anything with the framework?

Problem

How do you make sure you address all the audiences for the framework documentation?

Approaches

The problem with audiences comes down to simply time and money. Trying to create and maintain all these different documents can be a nightmare. It is expensive, and it is difficult to convince the team developing the framework that there is a problem. You will hear the argument, "The documentation is good enough for developing the framework, so it should be good enough to develop applications with the framework." If you decide the documentation is good enough when it's not and you ship it, you'll find that the learning curve for your framework is large and acceptance is slow. People may love the framework once they understand it, but you've made it very difficult for them to understand. Don't forget, however, that documentation can be added over time. If you get the tradeoff wrong—or simply don't have the funds for the documents—you can create better documentation later. However, be careful not to leave too much documentation until later; otherwise, you may impact customer reaction and acceptance of the framework. Remember that first impressions last the longest.

Make sure it is clear who the audience is for each of your documents. This allows the author of the document and the reader of the document to understand what its focus is. Be explicit. If the document was developed for framework developers, say so—and say why this might be a problem (or a benefit). In our clothing framework, our programming guide can state that it was written for developing the framework and as such some of the examination point support it encourages may be more than is needed when developing an application. Sometimes it is possible to partition a document to support the needs of multiple audiences—perhaps by providing visual cues or hiding some detail behind hyperlinks if the document is delivered in an online format. Be careful about overusing this approach, however; you can very easily create a single comprehensive document that no one can use effectively and that everyone hates!

When developing the IBM SanFrancisco project's user guides we used visual cues. These user guides provided domain information about the framework at varying levels ranging from executive overviews down to detailed analysis models meant to be read by skilled domain experts. Since all users of these guides were interested in the same information but at different levels, this approach worked well, since users could decide how deeply they wished to dive into any particular topic. Such an approach probably wouldn't work as well for a technical guide developed for both framework developers and application developers—their needs are sufficiently different that you are likely to confuse and frustrate both audiences with a combined document.

Another way to reduce the need for multiple documents is to provide education. However, this may not provide large savings. If the class is based on documents targeted at the wrong audience, the class won't be of much value. The only advantage will be for non-computer-based training, since the instructor will be present to answer these type of questions—if the class members have enough experience to know to ask the questions.

A better way to reduce the need for multiple documents is to provide consulting. Framework developers (both technical and domain experts) become framework consultants. They go out and work with customers to map from their applications to the framework. The consultants' detailed knowledge of the framework allows them to quickly identify which portion of the framework should be used and how it should be used. Consulting is an ideal opportunity to capture the information that needs to go into documentation while being paid to do so. If the developers on the consulting team and on the development team exchange roles at each release, the consultants can bring customer experience back to framework development and the developers can bring knowledge of the latest release out to the customer.

A problem with producing the audience-specific documents, mentioned above, is that you may not have the perspective to write them. In our consulting scenario above, the customer engagements are used to capture this information. If you don't do this, or if you need to be able to provide the documents immediately with the product, you'll need to use a different approach. For example, you could have an internal samples team that produces a framework sample or you could partner with a customer to use a beta release to capture this information. No matter how you capture this documentation, we recommend being prepared to iterate on the documentation and to actively solicit feedback from your customers.

In some cases you may need to layer the documentation. If you produce an international general ledger framework, you'll discover that there are five main generally accepted accounting principles (GAAPs) you should support. Each of these GAAPs comes with a different domain perspective. Writing a document that explains the framework from each of these perspectives would be expensive—not only in time but also in hiring experts in each GAAP. The solution is to layer the documentation. Pick the GAAP that most people in your target market will understand—for example, the U.S. GAAP—and provide it in such a way that other GAAPs can be added in the future. To do this, create a guide for what the framework provides (in framework terminology), then add information related to the U.S. GAAP (in U.S. GAAP terminology), showing how it maps to the framework. This allows someone (either you or a customer) to add a European GAAP document that also rests on top of the framework document. Ideally you would provide all five GAAP documents, but by including at least one key GAAP document, you give the members of your domain audience a way to view the framework from a perspective they understand so they can see how the domain maps to the abstract framework. This goes a long way toward helping users in other GAAPs understand the framework, and it enables information on other GAAPs to be added as time (and funds) permit.

Solution

- You can't afford to address all possible audiences.
  - You have to make a tradeoff about whom you will address and how much money you will spend.
  - This can change over time—you can always add more documentation.
- In the document, be explicit about who the document's audience is, with an explanation of what this means (both good and bad ramifications).
- Consider supporting multiple audiences with a single document.
  - Provide visual cues or hyperlinks to highlight or hide certain information.
  - Be sure that your audiences are similar enough to not be confused or frustrated by this approach.
- Education can be a substitute for extensive documentation. However, classes may not provide much cost savings, and their success depends on the interactions between teachers and students.
- Consulting can be a substitute for customers having to learn and understand everything, and it provides opportunities for feedback for documentation and development.
- You may not have the perspective to write the document.
  - You may not have the necessary expertise or experience.
  - You may need to get feedback through samples teams or early partnerships with customers.
- Consider layering the documentation, which allows piecewise expansion.

When to Use/Not Use

How (and whether) you use these approaches depends on the scope of your framework. If your framework is very focused, this may not be an issue. For example, if you are supporting only U.S. general ledgers, you wouldn't need to layer the documentation as described above. The broader the framework (and the larger the number of users), the more the use of such approaches becomes an issue.

Be aware of what already exists. If you can simply reference an existing document, this will save you a lot of time. For example, the IBM SanFrancisco project began before the existence of Enterprise JavaBeans (EJB), so it defined its own distributed object infrastructure. Thus documentation of this infrastructure had to be written. If EJB had existed, the IBM SanFrancisco project would have built on EJB[3] and would not have had to document the underlying distributed object infrastructure—instead, the framework user could go into any bookstore and buy documentation by the pound.

Applicability

- You have to look at what is best for your particular project. As the framework broadens, so does the audience—and the problem.
- Take advantage of documentation that already exists.

Known Uses

In addition to the examples already described, we applied most of the solutions over the lifetime of the IBM SanFrancisco project. For example, we made the tradeoff between documenting for all possible audiences and delivering the framework. Because the framework was something new, we decided that it was more important to go ahead and release the framework rather than delay it in order to wait for the documentation. We later added documentation. Also, when we defined the development artifacts, we were clear about the audience and the purpose of the artifacts. For example, the requirements were oriented toward the domain expert and framework development.

Related Patterns

None

---

3. IBM as part of WebSphere Business Components (http://www.ibm.com/software/webservers/ components) is harvesting the IBM SanFrancisco project components to provide business content based on EJB.

Chapter

8

Social Aspects

We began the main body of our book by elaborating on patterns that span the entire development process. Like the other bookend around our more detailed patterns for various development phases, we close the framework development discussion with more broadly applicable patterns, this time focusing on important social considerations that affect framework development. The best development processes, techniques, and skilled personnel are still likely to fail if team structure and interpersonal communication between team members are ignored. Some helpful patterns to consider when building development teams include

- There Is No "I" in Team (Section 8.1)—focusing on team dynamics, principles, and values
- The Great Communicator (Section 8.2)—recognizing the importance of someone who can speak both domain and technical languages
- Consistency Czar (Section 8.3)—making sure that consistency is preserved throughout the framework without overly constraining team members

We describe these three patterns in this chapter.

8.1 There Is No "I" in Team

Also Known As

The Importance of Team Dynamics

Intent

Organizational structure and dynamics are crucial to the success of any sizable development project, both at the project level and within individual teams participating in the project. Each team should be given time to establish its own style and approach within the broader constraints established for the project.

Context

If you have played organized team sports (especially in the United States, land of sports clichés), you have probably heard the title of this chapter used by at least one coach during a motivational talk. While the saying itself is trite, the meaning behind the saying is very important: a group of disconnected individuals, no matter how skillful, is likely to be less effective than another group working together as a team to reach a shared objective. You have probably experienced what it's like to work with a brilliant but challenging coworker. Perhaps this coworker felt he had to have the last word on every decision, perhaps he denigrated others' opinions to elevate his own, or perhaps he created dissent among the group by always favoring one person's viewpoint. Regardless of the method, he broke down team interactions and created an environment where individuals felt they had to fend for themselves instead of working toward common team objectives.

Building a team takes time. Whenever people come together in a group for the first time, a sorting-out period typically occurs during which people establish how they fit into the group.[1] Making sure that the sorting-out period results in a strong team structure instead of a fragmented bunch of individuals and cliques is one of the most important jobs that project leaders have during the early phases of any project. We specifically mention project leaders here to differentiate from the team leader role. *Project leaders* have a broader scope of responsibility for major portions of the entire development project

---

1. The stages a typical team goes through are *forming, storming, norming,* and *performing* [Scholtes 96].

and thus are responsible for establishing strategic project structure and organization. *Team leaders* have more focused responsibilities oriented toward a small group of team members assigned responsibility for some aspect of the project.

Example

One of the selection experts working on our clothing framework is well known in the clothing industry and has an ego to match. He constantly undercuts the other experts on the project and has established his own group of insiders who agree with everything he says. Morale on the team is down and going lower, and several domain experts and developers have privately told you that they're considering looking for other jobs.

Problem

Team dynamics are as important a factor to a project's success or failure as the skills brought to the team by individual members. How can project leaders establish a foundation for well-functioning team dynamics that can be built upon and maintained throughout the life of a project?

Approaches

Core values and principles need to be established up front by project leaders. Some elements that we've found to be effective in every team we've established include those listed below.

- **Do the right thing**. Set an expectation of action instead of a passive "wait to be told what to do" approach throughout the project. We're not advocating anarchy with this principle. Instead, we're encouraging you to establish an environment in which people feel free to make decisions based on incomplete information, then evaluate those decisions as the project progresses and more information becomes available [Beck 00].

- **Encourage latitude**. Establish broad working parameters within which each team member has extensive flexibility. While we believe that individuals need clear objectives established, we also believe that those individuals should be given considerable latitude in meeting those objectives. For example, if your test cases don't ship with the product, the clear objective would be that the developers must completely test their code, but your latitude could be that they don't have to meet the same coding standards or code reviews required for framework code. Framework development does add additional constraints beyond other software development because of the need for consistency throughout the framework's artifacts (see the Consistency Czar pattern, Section 8.3, for additional discussion on encouraging latitude and freedom of action within a scaffolding that preserves consistency).

- **Reward team successes.** While recognizing individual skills and accomplishments is important, we believe that team accomplishments should take priority. After all, no one individual can build the product you've been assigned to deliver. For example, an interchange of ideas within a team serves to harden and improve what often starts out as fuzzy ideas about a concept or topic. Use your imagination when rewarding the team. Although everyone appreciates money, also look for fun activities that encourage team building—activities that are different enough from people's jobs that team members won't take the activity too seriously and will focus on having fun (and hopefully building some "team lore" in the process). This doesn't mean that you can't recognize individuals, only that the team should be rewarded first.

When given a basic structure established by project leadership, teams with a core of experienced members will often form themselves. Individual team members will naturally gravitate toward their areas of expertise and will also fill gaps within the team that are aligned with their personalities and interests. For example, most teams of any size need a "jack-of-all-trades" who is willing and able to deal with the many miscellaneous items that come up over the course of a development project. Someone who has a curious nature and loves to learn new things will often step into this role in quick order.

Preexisting relationships between members of a new team can be both positive and negative. If handled well, these relationships can get the team off to a great start because these members already know and (hopefully) respect one another and also know how to work effectively with each other. However, you need to be aware of the dangers involved in this situation. If this sub-group doesn't actively work to include other members of the team, it's very easy for divisions to form. Project leaders can counteract this potential problem by working quickly to establish a broader project culture that builds from the core team's past experience, integrating its own inside jokes and traditions with those that already exist. For example, Tor's Second Cousin (see Section 4.2) became an inside joke among those of us working on the IBM SanFrancisco frameworks in Germany. As the business framework development moved back to the United States, we made sure to quickly explain the context behind this joke to new team members so they could understand our references and take part themselves in the joke.

You will also find that, when developing nontechnical software, teams composed of both domain experts and software developers bring at least two distinct cultures and working approaches to the project. Consider the situation we had in the early days of working on the IBM SanFrancisco project: a mix of software developers from the United States, Germany, and France, accounting domain experts from the United Kingdom and Germany, and warehousing logistics experts from all over Scandinavia. We had a considerable challenge creating a sense of team across these broad groups, dealing both with the members' jobs and their country-based backgrounds. On one team we had a domain expert from Germany working with a technical lead from the United States. The domain expert was a successful accountant who had been working in accounting for over 30 years. The technical lead had 10 years of programming experience. The technical lead knew nothing about accounting and the domain expert knew nothing about object-oriented programming. Luckily the accountant spoke English—otherwise, they wouldn't have had anything in common!

Individual idiosyncrasies come into play here. Often these idiosyncrasies are what make a particular developer or domain expert valuable to the team since they allow that person to bring a unique perspective to discussions that ultimately improve the end product. For example, even though the German accountant felt strongly that things should be done a certain way (one not involving abstraction), he brought much-needed experience with accounting to the project. Eventually he came to a point where he even tolerated the abstractions!

However, don't confuse idiosyncrasies with antisocial or disruptive behavior. Although most people want to be part of a success and are motivated to make that success happen, you will encounter people who are more interested in personal success or in looking good than in making the entire team successful. Such people can be extremely disruptive to team dynamics, and you can't ignore the problems they can cause. Hopefully you will be able to convince such individuals to consider the benefits to the project (and ultimately to themselves) of working more effectively with others. However, if you are unable to reach this point, remember that no one individual is essential to project success. You are likely to be better off removing a disruptive person from your project, no matter how skilled he or she is, than accommodating that person's unreasonable demands. There will be times when that approach isn't an option. In those situations, you need to "isolate the disease," preventing it from infecting the organization as a whole. Some techniques to consider when confronted with this situation include those noted below.

- Learn to work around the person by compromising on secondary issues and making sure he or she "wins" on those issues publicly.
- Isolate the person from those who react most strongly to him or her, for example, by ensuring that two individuals are never in the same meetings.
- Place the person in more of a consulting role that involves less direct personal interaction and more interaction through documentation.

Finally, you can overcome many operational difficulties within your teams if your core project leadership works well together. When team members see their leaders able to argue differing points with each other without getting personal or see leaders admitting their errors or inadequate understanding of an issue, this sends a powerful message to everyone working on the project. Team members working in such an environment feel confident that if they are involved in a disagreement with someone else on the team, they could bring that disagreement to the core group and get a fair evaluation. Such behavior sets an example of working well together that spreads out into the organization. In the end, it's up to project leadership to establish what's important to the project and to keep the team focused on the ultimate goal—delivery of a project that meets all stated objectives on time and within the allotted budget. When reminded of this objective, most team members will realize that "getting their way" is not that important in the grand scheme of things.

Solution

- Establish core project values and principles early in the project.
- Allow experienced team members to find their best fit within the project while making sure that all project needs are properly addressed.
- Take advantage of preexisting relationships between project members to give the project a jump start. However, be aware of the potential for divisive cliques to form from such relationships.
- Be sensitive to the different perspectives that domain experts and software developers bring to a project.
- Take advantage of team members' idiosyncrasies—their fresh perspectives will often improve the resulting product.
- Don't allow prima donnas to disrupt your team, no matter how talented they are.
  - Encourage them to change their behavior for the good of the team and project.
  - If necessary, remove them from your project.

– When you aren't allowed to remove a prima donna, work to minimize the disruption he or she causes to the project.

• Establish good working relationships between project leaders.

• As project leaders, set positive examples of teamwork that others can observe and follow.

When to Use/Not Use

Team dynamics are always important. As a project leader, pay most attention to establishing strong dynamics early in the project. In particular, a fun event can allow team members to express their personalities in a safe environment away from work, giving other team members a chance to build relationships that will be valuable to the team as the project progresses. Once you have established a good team structure, make sure you maintain it by paying attention to how individuals interact with each other on a regular basis.

Applicability

• On projects that involve more than two or three developers, you need to pay attention to team dynamics.
  – Smaller projects can often work with looser structures when establishing team relationships because individuals work on a daily basis with most if not all other project members.
  – Larger projects typically need more structure, with individual teams establishing their own identities within the context of the larger project.

Known Uses

As you might expect, team dynamics have played an important part of every project in which we've participated.

Related Patterns

• Tor's Second Cousin (Section 4.2)—care must be taken to ensure that inside jokes such as those that can result from applying the Tor's Second Cousin pattern quickly expand to include the entire organization.

• Consistency Czar (Section 8.3)—framework development adds additional constraints on developers because of the need for consistency throughout the framework's artifacts.

8.2 The Great Communicator

Also Known As

Translating between Domain and Technical Terminology and Concepts

Intent

Domain and technical terminology continues to become increasingly specialized. In order for information to be effectively transferred between domain analysts and technical developers, someone on your development team needs to be able to translate between the two groups and their distinct languages.

Context

If you've ever traveled to a country where you didn't speak the native language, you probably spent a lot of time being confused and frustrated, making guesses as to what was going on and how to do the things you needed to do. Occasionally you picked up hints along the way—maybe you saw a word that looked familiar (and, if you're lucky, actually meant what you thought it did instead of something completely different), perhaps you figured out how to pay your bus fare by watching how the locals did it for a while. It was hard work, and you knew that you were missing out on a lot of information. You were just getting by and making mistakes along the way, some inconsequential and some that may have been very important.

Let's bring a friend into the picture, a native who is fluent in both your language as well as the language of the country you're visiting. Now you can start to really communicate with others and take advantage of information and situations that you had no hope of grasping before. Through your friend you can engage in conversations with others, asking questions about things you find interesting and in turn telling them a bit about yourself and answering their questions. Over time, you might even start to learn the language from your friend, or at least some useful words and phrases that help you communicate more effectively.

This scenario is much like what confronts software developers assigned to work on a project in a business domain in which they have no background (and conversely, what domain experts have to deal with when they talk to software developers). New terminology and acronyms are used in rapid succession, people get in arguments about fine points of a topic that you haven't even begun to grasp, and in general you are totally overwhelmed with information that you can't process even though you know it will be important to you as you do your job. You need someone who can speak your language and can interpret the language of the "foreigners" you've just encountered, be they domain experts or software developers.

Example

You've just joined the clothing framework team as a software designer assigned responsibility to lead the design work for the clothing repair portion of the framework. Your team leader has invited you to a working meeting with the domain experts responsible for laying out the requirements that you are to support through your design. As you walk into the conference room, two domain experts are deep in discussion (some would say argument, but we'll give them the benefit of the doubt) over the relative merits of two repair techniques for fine wool cloth. One expert insists on interweaving as the only technique that is appropriate, while the other expert says that interweaving leaves the fabric too weak to stand up to extended use and that backfacing is the only approach that should be used in this case.[2] Sensing a pause in the conversation, you introduce yourself to the pair and, because you've just read about the Innocent Questions pattern (see Section 3.2), you suggest that perhaps a use of the Strategy design pattern [Gamma 94] might be appropriate, based on what you've heard thus far. They stare at you for a few seconds like you just said something in the lost language of the Incas (and from their perspective you might just as well have done so, since they didn't understand a word you said), then resume their "discussion."

Problem

Domain experts typically have little or no background or expertise in object-oriented software development, and in most cases object-oriented software developers similarly have at best a cursory knowledge of the business domain of their software project.

Approaches

Particularly in the early stages of a development project, you need to either find or quickly develop someone on the project team who is capable of serving as a translator between domain and technology concepts. This person doesn't necessarily need to become an expert in both areas; instead, it's been

---

2. All resemblance to actual fabric repair techniques in this example is entirely accidental.

our experience that people who aren't afraid to ask lots of innocent questions and who have a solid background in either the business domain or in object-oriented development often develop these translation skills quite quickly.

Sometimes a "big-brained" individual (see the Divide and Conquer pattern, Section 3.3) serving as lead architect comes into the project with strong technical and domain backgrounds. While hard to find, a person like this is ideal for bringing your entire project team rapidly up to speed in the areas where they have weaknesses. One word of caution, however: this approach will be successful only if the "big-brained" person is able to communicate with others while being aware of their sensitivities. As Alistair Cockburn states, "The ideal OO designer thinks abstractly, deals with uncertainty, communicates with colleagues" [Cockburn 98, p. 47]. It can be very frustrating to not understand concepts that others find elementary, and the last thing people in this situation need is to be made to feel ignorant. One effective approach to counter this feeling is to encourage individuals to restate what they've just learned in their own terms. This gives those individuals an opportunity to consolidate their thoughts and show growing expertise.

When there isn't a clear communicator, set up cross-education sessions during which the domain experts teach core domain concepts and the software developers teach the rudiments of object-oriented design and programming. These sessions not only help educate the team but also strengthen the team. By observing the interactions that occur during these education sessions, you also can begin to determine which individual (or individuals) seem to be best suited to take on the communicator role. For example, a domain expert who has done programming in the past may be a good choice, or perhaps a software developer who has had some experience (possibly some coursework in college) on the subject also has an engaging personality that brings out the best in others. Sometimes you just have to select someone to grow themselves into the role—usually one of the lead experts or designers.

Solution

- Find or develop someone on your project team who is capable of translating between domain and technical concepts. This might be a "big-brained" individual serving as lead architect, or it might be one or more people on your team who rapidly develop knowledge by asking lots of questions.

- Make sure that the translator or translators on your team are sensitive to individuals working to learn in the areas where they have no or limited background.

– Don't shut down questions by treating the questioner as stupid or incompetent.
– Encourage people to restate what they've just learned in their own terms.

When to Use/Not Use

Information transfer between technical and domain members of your team is always essential. If the developers don't understand what they have been asked to build to at least a basic level, they are very likely to introduce errors in the business logic being developed to support the requirements defined by the domain experts. Conversely, domain experts who understand at least basic object-oriented design principles can often suggest a design approach that might be successful in supporting a particular set of domain requirements.

However, you need to be aware of the potential damage that can result from the "consciously competent" individual. The term *consciously competent* comes from a theory of learning [O'Connor 93, Dennison 90] that states an individual goes through four stages of learning when encountering information that is new to him or her (see Figure 8.1).

1. **Unconsciously incompetent**: the individual doesn't understand how much he doesn't know. He may assume that, because he is an intelligent individual, he will be able to quickly learn this new information, thus underestimating the difficulty involved in developing new skills in this area. For example, when learning how to play a new game, you read through the rules (or have someone tell you the "important" ones) and

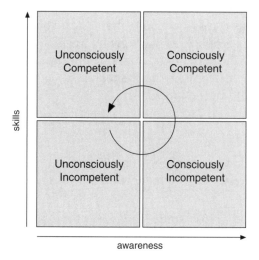

Figure 8.1 *Four stages of competence in learning*

you start playing. You think you know how to play, but you lose because you keep running up against the limits of your knowledge.

2. **Consciously incompetent**: after spending some time attempting to learn the new information, the individual realizes that he has greatly overstated the ease of learning the new topics and has a long way to go. At this stage, the individual is starting to learn basic principles, is probably able to point out areas where he needs to learn more, and is able to ask good questions about the topics he doesn't understand. In the game example, you know you're not clear on certain areas of the rules, so you refer to the rulebook and ask your friend who is very familiar with the game how to handle certain situations.

3. **Consciously competent**: the individual has learned quite a bit about the new area and is able to apply that information in many situations. In some cases it can be a great effort for the individual to apply his new knowledge, and he is still likely to make mistakes in more complex areas. In the game example, you know all but the most unusual rules, and you have begun to focus on learning and developing strategies for playing the game more effectively.

4. **Unconsciously competent**: at this stage, the individual has become a true expert in the new information. He is able to apply his knowledge rapidly and easily in most if not all situations where it is required. In the game example, you no longer think about the rules, you just know how to play.

Individuals in the "consciously competent" stage of learning often prematurely believe they have reached the "unconsciously competent" stage before they have in fact done so. Such individuals often assume they know more about domain or object-oriented development principles than they do in reality and can make poor decisions as a result because they don't confer with others more skilled or with more experience on the topic in question. It's crucial to validate the work done by individuals throughout the development process to ensure that these types of decisions don't sneak into your framework (see the Alles in Ordnung pattern, Section 3.1).

Applicability

- This pattern should be applied whenever the domain for which the software being developed isn't one in which the developers themselves have experience.
- In addition, it can be applied across software engineering disciplines (for example, in establishing good communication between software developers and software testers).

Known Uses

Development of the IBM SanFrancisco frameworks is a prime example of this pattern in action. Because of the wide-ranging scope of the project, numerous people served as "great communicators" on various aspects of both domain and object-oriented skills, information, and techniques.

Related Patterns

- Alles in Ordnung (Section 3.1)—validate development work during framework development process checkpoints to ensure that poor decisions made by less experienced individuals are caught and corrected.
- Innocent Questions (Section 3.2)—asking good questions is a key part of facilitating communication between technical and domain experts.
- Divide and Conquer (Section 3.3)—"big-brained" individuals with both technical and domain backgrounds can be ideal great communicators if they also have sufficient people skills.

8.3 Consistency Czar

Also Known As

Making Sure Consistency Happens

Intent

Without consistency, a framework's usability will be greatly reduced. This consistency will not occur naturally—someone needs to make sure it happens.

Context

Imagine that Rod Serling[3] has just come around the corner and placed you into a situation where the laws of physics continually change. One moment you feel as if you weigh 500 kg and you can barely move, and the next

---

3. The host of an old television program in the United States called *The Twilight Zone*. This show presented a series of seemingly normal situations in which the protagonist, a typical person, was confronted with a surreal or startling inconsistency within an otherwise normal situation—something that broke expected rules of behavior or other norms of society.

moment you have to hold onto something anchored to the ground because otherwise you might float away. As you look in one direction, you see things in the familiar visible color frequency spectrum, but when you look the opposite way, all you can see is infrared radiation. Naturally, you are going to be very cautious about making sudden moves, and in fact, you might even be paralyzed with fright, afraid to make any move whatsoever because of the potentially dire consequences that could arise. If you had an "enforcer" to make Rod go away (or even better, to keep him from showing up in the first place), your life would immediately return to normal and you would know what to expect from everyday situations.

The scenario we just described is obviously unrealistic, but in some small way, being asked to use a framework developed without consistency guidelines is similar. You approach each portion of the framework not knowing what to expect, discovering that two seemingly identical situations are handled entirely differently. Just as you begin to become comfortable in one area, you have to move to another area to complete the implementation of some domain process, and what you find there has no relationship or similarity to what you just left. You may run into inconsistencies in naming, in implementation idioms (like when to log or surface errors), in design techniques, or even in object granularity. Not a recipe for rapid application development and deployment—which, after all, is what frameworks are supposed to be good at supporting.

As we discussed with the Consistency Is King pattern (see Section 3.4), framework consistency is an iterative process involving four distinct phases: identification, specification, education, and enforcement. This chapter focuses on the enforcement phase of consistency. (Because enforcement doesn't happen in a vacuum, and because part of the enforcement process involves iteratively modifying consistency guidelines, this chapter also discusses the other three phases of framework consistency to some extent in the context of enforcement.) Even with all the best intentions in the world, if we don't manage and enforce consistency to some degree, the end result will be an inconsistently documented, designed, and implemented framework—a software equivalent to the *Twilight Zone* world described above.

Example

Let's revisit our example from the Consistency Is King section. The example described two portions of the framework (clothing selection and clothing repair) that had similar extensibility requirements, but our framework developers designed and implemented these sections inconsistently—in one case, they encapsulated the algorithm within a Strategy class [Gamma 94], and in the other case, they directly implemented the algorithm in the domain class. This creates confusion for users of our framework. If framework users first encounter the selection section of the framework, they will expect to see similar flexibility built into the repair section (and they will be frustrated when they find that to do what they need to do they have to do more work to overcome the restrictions of the framework). On the other hand, if they first deal with the repair section of the framework, they might not even consider looking for additional flexibility in the selection section because of their past experience with the framework.

Problem

Developers tend to be consistent within their own work, but giving framework developers complete freedom in designing and implementing their portions of the framework results in inconsistency across the framework.

Approaches

Enforcing consistency within a framework development project is a bit like juggling raw eggs—clamping down too tight will "crack the eggs" and prevent developers from fully implementing the full flexibility and extensibility that framework users want and need, and not defining sufficient restrictions will result in "eggs everywhere," a framework that is hard to use and perhaps even incomprehensible. In either case, we will have a big mess to clean up.

How can project leaders establish the right balance between freedom and restrictions? In other words, what has to happen to define and manage the enforceable consistency rules for a framework throughout the development life cycle of that framework? Here are some guidelines we've found useful when leading development projects.

Establish core guidelines early in the project. Nothing is worse than trying to lead (or work on) a project with no direction. Project leaders need to spend sufficient time early in the project life cycle establishing core guidelines for team members to follow. These guidelines shouldn't be defined in great detail; instead they should establish the basic "rules of the road" for domain experts and developers. In effect, this is a variation on the Something Is Better Than Nothing pattern (see Section 5.2), where instead of documenting what we know about the problem domain of our project, we document what we know about how to develop software based on our understanding of team dynamics, project size, and so on. Focus your guidelines on areas of framework development that directly affect what framework users see and work with. Some examples of guidelines that fall into this category and that we believe should be established early include class, method, and attribute naming conventions; general rules on size of component categories (for example, number of contained classes); and the set of standard design patterns (those you've had experience with in the past that you believe will be useful for this project) that should be considered when designing portions of the framework.

Don't agonize over details at this point; you are sure to get most of the details wrong because the project is at such an immature stage. Instead, make sure that everyone on the project understands the guidelines you have established and also understands their responsibilities within the scope of these guidelines—namely to help flesh out the guidelines with specific examples resulting from their development work on the framework and to identify and bring forward situations that appear to contradict existing guidelines.

Document guidelines through a combination of formal and informal means. Make sure that team members understand what they are supposed to do and not do in the course of development by clearly specifying places they can go to learn about framework guidelines. We've found it useful to combine formal means of documentation (for example, a design cookbook that grows throughout the project and is kept current by project architects) with informal means (for example, one-on-one mentoring and coaching by team leaders and architects). Here we have a variant on the Souvenirs pattern (see Section 7.1), where we are writing down just enough information to let us get our immediate job done, allowing us to revisit and codify this information at a later point as needed. Don't get carried away with getting every detail formally documented—it's more important to get the broad concepts captured so that individuals will at least be prompted to ask the necessary questions to apply the rules.

As an example, let's look at how we chose to document guidelines for the IBM SanFrancisco frameworks development team. When deciding how to document these guidelines, we often looked at how often the guideline (or pattern) would be applied by developers. Guidelines that were used frequently we were more likely to formally document. Infrequently used guidelines, or guidelines that were generated by the code generator, were lightly documented. In cases where it wasn't clear how heavily used a rule would be, we started out with lightweight documentation since it was easy to add more as more uses were discovered. For example, we rarely documented a potential pattern before we discovered a second or third use of the pattern. Pattern discovery and refinement is described in more detail in the Missed It by That Much pattern (see Section 6.2).

Assign clear responsibility and accountability for defining and enforcing guidelines. Consistency won't happen on its own. Responsibility for consistency has to be assigned. Although this can be done in a number of ways, our experience is that project architects (both domain and technical) should clearly have final responsibility and accountability for framework consistency. However, these individuals should not be given sole ownership; instead, they need to work with the various team leaders on the project to define and enforce framework development guidelines. Why is this important? Because the individual team leaders are in touch with the day-to-day realities of what the development team is confronting. Two of the most important responsibilities in their role are to serve as the initial sounding board for further guideline development and also to discover situations where existing guidelines are falling short.

However, because team leaders are likely to have a more narrow view of the framework than the architects do, it's important to involve architects in guideline refinement. Architects have the breadth of vision over the entire framework to understand whether a particular situation is an isolated case that can be dealt with in a "one-off" manner or whether the essence of the situation needs to be abstracted into a new or refined development guideline. Cross-leader interaction is also crucial here to "get it right"—each team leader has a different background and has seen different situations on the current project, and each should be ready to contribute his or her viewpoints to the guideline definition process.

Be prepared to adapt and extend guidelines gradually as the project matures. Nothing makes a person smarter than experience. As we've already mentioned, your team leaders will see different situations arise during framework development, and as a result they will begin to formulate rule extensions and new rules with their team members. This is exactly what you want to occur; allowing rules to grow from experience helps to prevent an overly restrictive development environment.

Over the course of framework development, some newly proposed rules will contradict rules that are already in place. Don't dismiss these rules out of hand; in many cases they should be incorporated into the rule set. In particular, remember the What, Not How pattern (see Section 4.3) and make sure you understand the problem the proposed rule is trying to solve. Sometimes these proposed rules come out of misunderstandings of domain or design topics; once this misunderstanding is resolved, the need for the rule evaporates. Once you have determined that the proposed rule is valid, evaluate its effect on current development work. In other words, exercise judgment as to when the new rule should be applied. Some proposed rules may be so drastic in nature that they need to be rejected for the current project—consider those rules hard-earned knowledge that you can and should apply to your next project. Other rules may be important enough to incorporate into the current project but would be too disruptive to apply at the current time. Perhaps your project has a near-term deadline that you must meet, or perhaps making changes to lower layers of the framework would cause too much disruption to other higher-level framework categories currently under development. These rules can be held in abeyance until the next planned major framework iteration. Other rules may have more limited impact on the existing parts of the framework that can be absorbed by the development teams as part of the normal development process. Judgment comes into play as to when new consistency guidelines should be applied to the framework-in-progress—as always, tradeoffs between correctness, expediency, and other business and technical issues arise. Remember that the best is the enemy of the good, and make sure that you don't paralyze your development team by constantly introducing new and contradictory guidelines.

Don't overspecify rules and guidelines. Just because you can define a rule doesn't mean that you should do so. Code formatting rules such as indentation and white space are typically overkill—it's quite easy to postprocess source code through a code formatter to bring consistency across code developed by different team members, and forcing a team member to code in a formatting style that he or she is uncomfortable with will be counterproductive at best and at worst will lead to the introduction of more bugs. Likewise, one can go "pattern crazy" at the design level and start forcing patterns where they don't belong. This is often known as the "hammer and nail" syndrome (from the aphorism "when you have a hammer, everything looks like a nail"), and it can be a trap for inexperienced teams new to patterns usage.

Make sure team members have areas where they have freedom to be completely creative within the broader restrictions of the framework. You might expect that some of your developers will chafe under the restrictions placed on them by your framework development guidelines. Most software developers consider what they do as art, and what you are trying to do by imbedding these guidelines into a structured development process is convert artists into engineers. How can you direct the artistic energy from your developers productively? We have two suggestions.

1. Encourage developers to identify situations that don't conform to existing rules and to define proposed solutions for those situations. Those proposed solutions are often the basis for new or adapted guidelines that can be broadly applied across the framework.

2. Give developers greater freedom in those parts of their job that don't directly affect what is delivered to the framework user. A prime example of this is unit test cases that developers build to test their code before they integrate that code into the broader framework. We find it helpful to establish a very lightweight scaffolding (that is, a testing framework) for unit test case development [Beck 02] that accommodates test case automation, then to allow developers to freely define how to apply that scaffolding to their specific code.

Solution

- Decide early in the development process what aspects of the framework need to be consistent and how to propagate the guidelines and rules that define consistency.
  - Consistency matters most in those artifacts of the framework that will be seen and worked with by framework users.
  - Don't try to define every situation up front; instead concentrate on broad guidelines during the initial phases of development.
  - Allow the guidelines to grow in a natural manner, even though this will probably lead to some level of iteration and rework for portions of the framework developed first.
- Document guidelines through a combination of formal and informal means.
  - Formal approaches include design cookbooks, lists of specified design patterns to be applied and the circumstances when they should be applied, and coding style samples.
  - Informal approaches typically involve one-on-one mentoring and coaching, for example, review sessions in which inconsistencies are pointed out by team leaders and alternative approaches described.
  - When it isn't clear that the guideline will be applied often, consider starting with informal documentation.
- Assign responsibility for enforcement of consistency guidelines. Team leaders should be made accountable to project architects and should work out with those architects the general consistency guidelines early in the project life cycle, refining those guidelines as needed as the project matures.
- Adapt consistency guidelines as the project matures by recognizing situations in which existing consistency guidelines need to be modified or extended. Understand the costs and benefits associated with modifying a guideline, and make an informed choice to reject, implement (consistently across the entire framework), or defer the proposed change to a future iteration of the framework.

- Don't overspecify consistency guidelines. Some guidelines are unnecessary and even counterproductive; make sure the guidelines you define provide real value so that you can easily justify them to your development team and not create needless frustration within the team.
- Give developers freedom within the consistency guidelines to be creative.
  - As part of the review process, encourage developers to bring forward for review situations they don't believe fit into the existing guidelines, with their proposed solutions.
  - Allow developers greater freedom in areas of development that will not be delivered to framework users (for example, unit test cases).

When to Use/Not Use

Small development projects usually do not require explicit consistency enforcement. In these cases the team developing the framework is usually small enough that good ideas naturally propagate among team members. Once a team grows beyond six to eight developers, however, the communication paths between developers become too extensive to maintain and their designs begin to diverge. At this point, it becomes important to introduce design and implementation guidelines and apply those guidelines throughout the review checkpoints incorporated into your development process.

Applicability

- Use judgment in how far to extend framework development guidelines.
  - Narrowly used frameworks and frameworks that are small in size require less rigorous definition and enforcement of framework guidelines.
  - Large frameworks, such as the IBM SanFrancisco frameworks, are heavily dependent on consistent design and implementation to increase the understandability and usability of the framework, and thus they more heavily rely on framework consistency rules and guidelines.

Known Uses

All development projects we have been involved in have established some form of consistency czar as part of the development structure. In the IBM San-Francisco frameworks, each team leader was responsible for ensuring that consistency rules were applied throughout the framework, and the team leaders along with the architects served as a core team to define and elaborate on the needed consistency rules.

Related Patterns

- Consistency Is King (Section 3.4)—framework consistency is an iterative process involving four distinct phases: identification, specification, education, and enforcement. The consistency czar is responsible for enforcement.

- What, Not How (Section 4.3)—make sure you understand the problem a proposed consistency rule is trying to solve; some proposed rules come out of misunderstandings of domain or design topics and are not valid.

- Something Is Better Than Nothing (Section 5.2)—early in the project, document what you know about how to develop software based on your understanding of team dynamics, project size, and so on.

- Missed It by That Much (Section 6.2)—start with lightweight documentation when beginning to define a potential pattern, then flesh it out more formally if the pattern truly exists and can be exploited by your project.

- Souvenirs (Section 7.1)—document just enough guideline information to get the immediate job done. Revisit and codify this information at a later point as needed.

Chapter

9

Framework Use

Before a framework can provide value, someone has to use the framework, customizing and augmenting it to make an end-user application. As with any software development project, the application's requirements and use cases are the starting point for this process. What is unique when using frameworks is that instead of simply moving to the next phase of development, a mapping step is added where you look to see what's available in the framework that can be used to fulfill your needs. Patterns that will assist you in using a framework include

- Just Learn It (Section 9.1)—spending time up front learning about the framework
- Map Early, Map Often (Section 9.2)—mapping to the framework early and frequently to expand possibilities for reuse
- Color Inside the Lines (Section 9.3)—customizing a framework only where it is necessary

In this chapter, we discuss these patterns for framework use.

9.1 Just Learn It

Also Known As

Using Frameworks Requires Up-Front Education

Intent

Frameworks, unlike other reusable software, cannot be picked up and immediately used. Frameworks require up-front learning. This learning can and should be staged.

Context

The first time you drove a car, did you walk up, get in, and drive off? Probably not; you had to learn some things before you were able to start driving. You had to learn how to control the car and you had to learn the core rules of the road. Both areas of education were necessary. Without this up-front learning, your first experience in a car might still have been all right—you might have gotten lucky—or it might have been a disaster. Using a framework is very similar to this. You need to do some up-front learning in order to use it properly. Just like learning to drive a car, you don't have to learn it all at once. You start with the core of the framework (the car's controls), learn the way it addresses problems (the rules of the road), and then you can get started. This gives you a foundation from which you can understand the domain content provided by the framework. Just like you wanted to get driving as soon as possible, the project deadlines will push you to stop learning and start applying. Finding the balance between spending all your time learning and applying what you've learned is a difficult problem.

Example

The clothing management framework comes with lots of documentation: user guides, requirements, uses cases, designs, and so on (see the Exposing It All pattern, Section 3.6). Where do you start? Do you have to read it all to use the framework? If you pick up the selection support and try to build a selection algorithm, you quickly find that you don't understand all the methods or all the parameters. For example, why are there multiple create signatures and when would you decide to use one versus the others? Wouldn't this be obvious from the interface documentation? It may or may not be, but it is unlikely. Normally things that are part of the programming model would not be documented at this level. The interface documentation assumes you are familiar with the programming model, so these things don't have to be explicitly documented. You may be tempted to argue that these should be documented as well as any other methods. You would win, but you have to be practical. You want your developers to document what is unique, long before you want them to document what is normal. In addition, even if you did win, it would likely be a Pyrrhic victory: there would be so much to wade through that the typical user would find it next to impossible to find the really important documentation.

Ultimately, however, you want to use only the selection portion of the clothing framework, and you don't want to have to learn the entire framework just to use this one piece. How should you go about doing this in the most efficient manner?

Problem

How do you trade off the need to learn the framework before you use it with the desire to start using it right away?

Approaches

Understanding a framework can be a challenging process. Developers are tempted to go straight to the interface documentation or source code and see what the framework does. A few developers are successful at this, but most get lost. Domain experts, on the other hand, look for things they understand, the business objects and processes with which they are used to working. Often this leads to major misunderstandings, either that the framework does something it doesn't do or that it doesn't do something it does. The framework's abstract names and overloaded meanings are land mines the domain expert has to avoid. How can you avoid these pitfalls?

If a framework is documented properly, it provides a number of entry points in its documentation (see the Give 'Em What They Want pattern, Section 7.2). These entry points allow you to understand the framework at different levels, ranging from executive-level summaries of the framework function all the way down to detailed design models and possibly even the source code. If you have this level of documentation, use it for all it's worth. Take advantage of the entry points to help get each team member to the information best suited for his or her needs. These entry points shouldn't limit access to the documentation; good documentation allows easy navigation. The entry points should guide you across all the framework's capabilities at a certain level, hiding the details and allowing you to grasp the bigger concepts of the framework first and then filling in the details at a deeper level. If a framework is poorly documented, you can still achieve the same result by disciplining yourself to review the framework's capabilities at the right level.

As you go through the documentation, you should keep a number of things in mind. Proper documentation makes these guidelines easier to follow, but it doesn't make them any less important. First of all, don't dip too deeply into the details of the framework when you are first trying to learn it. In the beginning it is very easy to lose the forest for the trees. Expect to make multiple passes over the framework documentation. Focus on creating a high-level mental map into which you can plug in details in subsequent passes. This doesn't mean you shouldn't look at the details. Use the details to help you understand—jumping into and out of them as needed.

For example, your first focus may be on the basic requirements met by the framework. As you begin to build a map of these requirements in your head, you might choose to dip more deeply into the analysis level for one portion of the framework (often the area you intend to use in your application's prototype or first iteration). Spend some time at that level, and then jump back up to the requirements. This allows you to get a feel for how these two layers of the framework documentation interact. You might then choose to fan out to another area of the framework to gauge how consistently the framework handles different areas of function, or you might choose to continue to drill into the area where you started, down to the design and implementation layers of the framework.

In any event, beyond the basic objective of learning the framework, you should also be looking for broader patterns of documentation in the framework. How do the different documentation layers interact? Are different areas of the framework documented consistently? If not, how do they vary? What abstractions are consistently present in the framework? Have these abstractions been documented as patterns (either new patterns or existing patterns)?

Keep in mind that you don't have to learn the entire framework to use it. Learning the core and the details of the portion (or portions) you plan to use allows you to use the framework more quickly. The key, though, is to come back and expand this knowledge so that you can take greater and greater advantage of the framework in subsequent projects (or iterations of your current project).

If you have a large project, you'll find it valuable to begin your project with a small core team building a prototype that uses the framework. This team should follow the above guidelines to learn about the framework during the process of building the prototype. In addition, the team members should be creating meta-documentation about how they learned and used the framework—in effect, creating a framework road map for the rest of the project team using terminology and style that is familiar to that team. Recognize that every development group has its own style and way of communicating, and it is very unlikely that the team that developed the framework has the same style as the team using the framework. If it does, great—the meta-documentation is easy to produce. Otherwise, the road map becomes quite important in speeding up the learning curve for subsequent users of the framework.

Make sure your prototype team contains strong developers and domain analysts who want the prototype to succeed. At least some of these developers and analysts should also be good communicators (see The Great Communicator pattern, Section 8.2), since you are going to use members of this team to seed other groups as part of fanning out the framework learning process throughout the larger organization.

Depending on how large your group is, you might even go so far as to turn this prototype into a set of formal education materials that walk new users of the framework through the development process, leading them to the same mapping, design, and implementation that the prototype team built. The IBM SanFrancisco project uses this approach within its documentation. One portion of each Core Business Process User Guide is dedicated to a case study that uses a portion of the framework to implement a prototype business process. This documentation covers the entire development cycle from requirements definition and mapping to the actual source code used to implement the prototype.

Don't forget to educate your management and executive team about your use of the framework. As in any form of reuse, using a framework may at first take more time than building from scratch. Your management team needs to understand that this near-term cost will result in a long-term benefit as more and more of the framework is reused and designing, coding, and testing are avoided. Involving managers in the prototype process at an appropriate level, or at least exposing them to the framework documentation in a digested form so they can understand what is going on in the learning process, will pay dividends as the project moves forward.

Solution

- If the framework is well documented, take advantage of the different audience-centric entry points.
- If the framework is not well documented, use discipline to review the available documentation in a more efficient way.

- Whenever reading the documentation:
  - Don't dip into the details too early.
  - Expect to make multiple passes.
  - Build high-level maps into which you can plug concepts.
  - Remember that you don't have to learn it all at once.
- Look for patterns of documentation, including the use of patterns within the framework.
- For large projects, establish a prototype framework usage team.
  - This prototype team should create meta-documentation to help the rest of team use the framework as the project progresses.
  - Make sure the team contains strong developers with good communication skills.
  - Use team members to seed the wider organization.
  - Use the prototype as a basis for educational materials for the development team.
  - Use the prototype as a tool for educating executives and managers on the near-term versus long-term benefits of using a framework.
- There will be an up-front learning cost. Make sure management knows you are trading off the near-term learning costs for the long-term savings that come with reuse.

When to Use/Not Use

If you can't (or won't) pay the up-front cost of learning the framework, you should consider other forms of reuse, such as coarse-grained components (see Appendix A) or class libraries.

Applicability

- A framework may not be right for you if you can't or won't do the up-front learning.

Known Uses

Although empirical data is not available, our observation was that the users of the IBM SanFrancisco frameworks who paid this up-front learning cost had a much greater success rate delivering completed applications built on the framework.

Related Patterns

- Exposing It All (Section 3.6)—frameworks that expose most of their details are likely to be easier to learn than those that hold back details.
- Give 'Em What They Want (Section 7.2)—different forms of documentation allow different types of users to have different entry points when learning the framework.
- The Great Communicator (Section 8.2)—use your prototype to build great communicators.

9.2 Map Early, Map Often

Also Known As

Use Frameworks by Mapping

Intent

In order to make the most of a framework, you should map to it throughout your development process. Once you've mapped, you should continue to refine that mapping.

Context

When you assemble something from a kit, such as a piece of furniture from a mail order company, do you look at the instructions? The instructions, depending on your level of experience assembling things, can provide a lot of valuable information on how to put the item together. They can recommend an order for putting things together that ensures you won't have leftover parts when you're done.

In some ways this is similar to using a framework. When we map to the framework, it is similar to checking the instructions. We're looking to see if there is something in the instructions that can help us finish the assembly. We may look at the instructions and find that there isn't anything useful, or we may find that they recommend an order that makes the assembly much, much simpler. We're reusing the knowledge captured in the instructions. The sooner we can reuse that knowledge, the more useful it is. This is like mapping to the framework—the process of going from what is needed by the application you're building to what the framework provides. Just like instructions, the sooner you discover something you can reuse, the better. If you look at the instructions after you're halfway through assembly, you may no longer be able to take advantage of a recommendation on assembly order.

While this analogy is useful, it only goes so far since assembly instructions are not reused from item to item—the chair assembly instructions don't help you assemble a lamp. For frameworks, mapping goes hand in hand with learning a framework (see the Just Learn It pattern, Section 9.1). Before you can map, you have to learn what the framework does. Once you know what the framework does, how do you map to it? You probably won't just do it naturally, especially when you first start using a framework.

Example

When we're developing a clothing selection application, we start with the requirements and use cases and then continue through the development process until the application is coded and tested. When do we take advantage of the framework? Normally, our developers think to look at the framework only when they remember something is there. If our development process doesn't explicitly include mapping steps throughout the process, we won't get the most reuse (and thus benefit) out of the framework.

Problem

How do you get the most benefit out of a framework, or at least make sure you make reasonable attempts to use framework functions?

Approaches

Mapping to framework functions must be discussed within the context of a methodical development process of some kind. This may or may not be similar to the framework development process described in the Alles in Ordnung pattern (see Section 3.1)—depending on how extensive your development project is, you may be using a more or less extensive process than that used by the framework developers. Regardless of which development process you choose, the process will allow you to add formal steps during which you actively look for things you can use from the framework—explicitly mapping your needs to what the framework provides.

Mapping early is important not only because it gives you the greatest reuse but also because it helps you align your thought processes with the framework.

For example, when trying to map you notice how the framework has broken down the problem. If the breakdown is appropriate for your needs, which hopefully it is, you can align yourself with that breakdown, making subsequent use of the framework much easier. If you don't do this, you may find yourself working at cross-purposes to the framework. For example, you might introduce a different partitioning that makes it harder to figure out whether the framework can be used, thus forcing you to modify the framework more extensively than you otherwise would have had to do.

Mapping at different levels often influences your iterative process. This causes you to refine or flesh out your original mapping. Refinement consists of finding out that a different piece of the framework provides the support you need, discovering that what you first thought the framework supported is in fact not supported, or discovering that mapping should have occurred earlier. Fleshing out involves taking the mapping to the next level. Often this includes determining which extension points you'll use and identifying how you can use them to fulfill your application needs.[1]

Mapping doesn't have to be concrete—a framework provides abstractions. In fact, these can be abstract enough to allow mapping to a new and possibly unexpected domain. For example, the IBM SanFrancisco Warehouse Management framework is being used to provide scheduling of post–acute care nursing [Jaufmann 00].

When you can't map to the framework, you will have to provide these pieces yourself. We recommend keeping a consistent style for the design (including patterns) and implementation of these pieces by following the approaches used by the framework.[2] This keeps the application consistent, so it is easier to maintain, and it makes subsequent mapping (as the framework supplies new elements and as new developers extend your application by using these pieces) much easier.

Solution

- Use a methodical development process. Add mapping steps to explicitly map from your needs to the framework.

- Map early, which aligns your application with the framework for greater reuse.

---

1. For a good example of the mapping process in action, see the *IBM SanFrancisco Warehouse Management User Guide*'s example application [IBM 99].

2. Keep in mind the potential for over-engineering discussed in the Color Inside the Lines pattern, Section 9.3.

- Mapping is iterative, including both:
  - Refinement: discovering further alignment (or misalignment) between the framework and your application
  - Fleshing out: taking the discovered mappings to a greater level of detail
- Mapping does not have to be concrete. Framework processes developed for one domain may be abstracted to support different domains through terminology and function mapping.
- When you have nothing to map to, stay consistent. Use framework approaches and patterns to build application-specific elements.

When to Use/Not Use

Often when mapping steps are not included in the development process, the framework becomes more like a class library—used only for detailed implementation.

How much and when you map is really up to you. Ideally you should map at each step of the development process, but doing some mapping (possibly at key steps) is better than no mapping at all.

Applicability

- Not mapping against a framework turns a framework into a class library.
- Mapping at some levels is better than no mapping at all.

Known Uses

Mapping techniques are used by customers in order to take advantage of the IBM SanFrancisco frameworks' capabilities. For example, as mentioned earlier, at one extreme a customer created a scheduling application for post–acute care nursing using the IBM SanFrancisco frameworks' Warehouse Management support [Jaufmann 00].

Related Patterns

- Alles in Ordnung (Section 3.1)—using a framework also requires a methodical development process, but one that may be different from the one used to develop the framework.

- Just Learn It (Section 9.1)—mapping is easier when you understand the framework.
- Color Inside the Lines (Section 9.3)—be consistent when using the framework, but don't overdo it.

9.3 Color Inside the Lines

Also Known As

Change Only What You Need to Change

Intent

Don't extend or use part of the framework just because you can. Limit yourself to extending and using only what's necessary.

Context

Renovating a house can be similar to using a framework. You want to ensure that you renovate only what you need to and no more. You also want to try to use standard renovation supplies and limit the need for specialized work—especially in areas where you might be doing further renovation. For example, if you decide to recarpet and repaint a room, you probably don't want to bother resurfacing the hardwood floor beneath the carpet. You would repair it if needed, but you wouldn't bother waxing and polishing it.

One reason to use a framework is to avoid reinventing the wheel. The framework you select should provide you with prebuilt entities and processes as well as ways for you to customize those prebuilt elements. Your goal should be to use the domain knowledge represented by these elements as much as possible, customizing the framework where you need to incorporate new algorithms, processes, or other elements. However, customization is a two-edged sword. First, you have to realize that every part of a framework you change has to be retested (against the framework and application) and is one more part you have to maintain over time. Second, many of the development techniques used by a framework, such as the patterns it incorporates, are oriented toward providing customizable software. This doesn't mean you shouldn't take advantage of these patterns and other extension points in the parts you have to create from scratch; it only means that you need to be aware how you use them. If you aren't, you may be adding unnecessary complexity.

Example

The IBM SanFrancisco frameworks provide built-in support for a pattern called class replacement [Carey 00]. This pattern allows reusable code to create a class, and then the user of that reusable code can change the actual class created—without having to modify the reused code. It is a variation of the Abstract Factory pattern from the *Design Patterns* book [Gamma 94]. Almost everything in the IBM SanFrancisco frameworks can be class-replaced. As you can guess, class replacement isn't free—there are overhead costs. Because the IBM SanFrancisco project is a framework, it was impossible for its developers to know which classes would need to be replaced and which wouldn't. Thus, this choice to make almost everything class-replaceable makes perfect sense. When developing your application code, however, you know what the final classes will be. If you know what the final class will be, it doesn't make sense to support class replacement for those classes. You should evaluate whether you really need class replacement and remove the support where it isn't needed.

Unfortunately, the IBM SanFrancisco project makes it easier to support (and use) class replacement than to omit the support. The frameworks provide a code generator that helps generate a large portion of the code from the design model. This generator supports generating classes only with class replacement. Thus you would need to modify the generated code or write the class from scratch to remove the support. This is indicative of the type of mistakes a framework can make in its documentation. Since all of the IBM SanFrancisco frameworks' classes need to be class-replaceable, the documentation in the programming model and the tooling describes (and supports) only this case.

This example also touches on the other aspect of changing only what needs to be changed. Everything in the IBM SanFrancisco frameworks supports class replacement, but this does not mean you, as a framework user, should class-replace everything in the framework. You need to understand and use class replacement when it is the appropriate technique. The IBM SanFrancisco frameworks provide documentation that describes this technique as well as alternatives, such as subclassing and aggregation, that can be used to extend class behavior plus the tradeoffs involved in using each technique.

Problem

Frameworks must be customizable in general since the developers don't know how the frameworks will be used. You are building an application that narrows the framework to a specific use—in effect, you are "tying up the loose ends" of the framework. How do you make sure you don't overuse framework extension points or copy framework development approaches inappropriately?

Approaches

The first approach is simply to understand the problem and the possibility that the framework documentation may be oriented more toward framework development and not application development. Beyond this you can build checkpoints into your review process (see the Alles in Ordnung pattern, Section 3.1). These checkpoints ensure that the right questions are asked.

- Does the framework really need to be changed here to do what you need?
- Can you do this differently and stay within the framework's customization approaches?
- Are you providing customizability that your application doesn't need?

In other words, focus on fulfilling your needs in a consistent manner that appropriately takes advantage of the framework.

Another key approach is to try to keep your customizations to the extension points identified by the framework. These extension points are designed to be well encapsulated, so making changes there should be less likely to perturb the rest of the framework. By "staying within the lines" established by the framework, you minimize your testing and maintenance burden dramatically, allowing you to focus your testing toward the encapsulated customizations you have made to the framework.

Another level of customization occurs at the category level. If the framework has defined facades (based on the Facade design pattern [Gamma 94]) around categories (that is, taken a component-based approach to framework elements), you can consider doing wholesale replacement of the implementation behind the facade. For example, if the Currency category is surrounded by a facade that allows currencies and exchange rates to be defined and used, you can replace it in its entirety, perhaps delegating this responsibility to a third-party service.

However, if the framework has not actually defined independent coarse-grained components, this approach can be risky—there may be unobserved relationships between portions of the framework that even the framework developers don't realize are present. For example, in the Currency category above, we may have provided an interface on the facade for converting from one currency to another using the defined exchange rate, but we might not have realized that we need an interface for retrieving the exchange rate (or rates) that were used to do the conversion.

In general, try to maintain contravariance rules whenever customizing a framework. This rule ensures that you are correctly fulfilling the class contracts.

However, there will be times when you need to break contravariance. (See the It's Still OO to Me pattern, Section 6.4, for a more detailed discussion.) When you do this, you will need to break it in a consistent manner throughout the framework. In other words, if you break contravariance rules with a class in the framework, you will need to search out every use of that class within the framework and ensure that you handle the change appropriately. In effect you are doing wholesale replacement of a set of interactions within the framework in parallel, and these replacements must be maintained in parallel. If you do this, make sure you carefully document what you are doing since it is very easy to come along later and not realize the impact of a change to one of the classes in this related "contravariance web."

Solution

- Be aware that a framework is focused on providing highly reusable software and you are providing a specific application.
- Add checkpoints to explicitly check that you are appropriately using the framework.
- Try to use extension points identified by the framework.
- You may be able to replace entire categories of framework function, but be aware of hidden dependencies.
- If you break contravariance within the framework, do it in a consistent manner.

When to Use/Not Use

Take the framework documentation as a guide for how you should do your own development, but don't take it as the final word. You have to look at what the framework provides in light of its goal to provide highly reusable software and compare that with what you need for the specific application you are writing. Don't be too quick, though, to go to either extreme. Don't just throw out everything the framework did and do your own thing for your code—you'll miss the opportunity to leverage a lot of knowledge in the framework, and you will introduce inconsistencies between your code and the framework code that will make future maintenance of your software more difficult. And don't blindly do what the framework does; it may be inappropriate for your circumstances and may add unnecessary processing or complexity. When changing framework elements, use the extension points provided by the framework except in the most extreme cases.

Applicability

- Just because the framework does something doesn't mean you should or shouldn't do the same thing. Use your requirements to evaluate whether a framework technique is appropriate for your particular case.

Known Uses

The IBM SanFrancisco frameworks users who applied this pattern were more able to absorb changes to the framework—both performance changes made as the framework evolved and structural changes resulting from migration of the IBM SanFrancisco frameworks content to the Enterprise Java Beans programming model.

Related Patterns

- Alles in Ordnung (Section 3.1)—just as checkpoints are valuable when developing frameworks, they provide useful opportunities for feedback during framework usage.
- It's Still OO to Me (Section 6.4)—if you're going to break contravariance, do it consistently.

Chapter
10

Conclusion

So, you've put up with our humor and our opinions and made it this far—you are to be congratulated for your perseverance! We hope you've gained some new and useful insights into framework and broader software development issues and that we've helped you consolidate some of those "gut feelings" you've developed over time as you've worked on software development projects.

You've likely noticed that much of our discussion revolves around the human aspects of software development. As we stated in the Alles in Ordnung pattern, the best development process in the world won't be effective unless the various members of your team are truly communicating and collaborating with each other throughout the development process. We believe that this view of the development process as a means to an end (in other words, define just enough process and no more) is a proper middle ground between those who believe that the process is paramount and those who believe software development is an art that can't be constrained by something as restrictive as a process.

Supporting this core belief, we feel strongly that planned communication between framework team members (as in the Where's Mr. Spock When You Need Him?, The Great Communicator, and Innocent Questions patterns) and between the framework and its users through its structure (as in the Divide and Conquer and Eating the Elephant patterns) and documentation (as in the Exposing It All, Souvenirs, and Give 'Em What They Want patterns) is essential to a successful and useful framework, one that users can rapidly learn and understand (as in the Just Learn It pattern). Another easily overlooked aspect of such communication is the importance of consistency throughout the framework (as in the Consistency Is King, That's the Way the Cookie Crumbles, Missed It by That Much, and Consistency Czar patterns).

You've probably noticed a few more themes throughout this book (themes that we laid out in Table 1.1, which is also printed on the inside back cover for easy reference). One theme is our expectation that iteration is a way of life in software, and particularly in framework development (see the Something Is Better Than Nothing, Eating the Elephant, Missed It By That Much, and Iterate, Iterate, Iterate patterns). Preparing for and even encouraging this iteration results in more rapidly developed and more resilient software. Framework users aren't immune from this trend, either—the mapping process (see the Map Early, Map Often pattern) ultimately involves iterating against the framework and its documentation throughout all stages of the application development process.

You also probably detected a theme around incompleteness, that is, the need to leave some things out of a framework that you would put into a piece of software developed specifically for an application. Patterns such as Tor's Second Cousin, The Stupid Test, and Pass the Buck discuss the tension between providing more complete function and leaving the framework open enough to allow its users to easily adapt it to their needs. Likewise, we discuss some key considerations to getting what you put into the framework right—keeping it flexible enough to make it useful—in the Innocent Questions, It Depends, and What, Not How patterns.

Last but not least, we put in what might seem to be obvious reminders—don't forget your object-oriented principles (It's Still OO to Me); pay attention to the people on your development team, without whom you won't have a product (There Is No "I" in Team); and if you're using a framework, really use it, don't work around it (Color Inside the Lines). In the rush to deliver software faster and faster with fewer and fewer people, it's easy to forget these basic rules.

Finally, remember that as a framework developer, you're not allowed to wear a bulletproof vest. More than any other type of software, the framework you build is fully exposed to the cruel, hard world; be ready for criticism and suggestions for improvement from all directions. Listen to this feedback with an open mind and put the "24-hour rule" into play whenever you feel your blood pressure start to rise. Sleep on it and assess the input with a fresh eye the next day. Underneath what initially feels like unfair criticisms, untrue allegations, and insulting innuendos there is very likely at least a germ of truth. Ultimately, listening to your framework users will give you key insights—insights that will help you both improve your existing frameworks and make your future framework development efforts better from the start.

Appendix

A

Frameworks and Components

We've alluded throughout this book to the notion of framework-based components. For example, in the Eating the Elephant pattern (see Section 5.1), we discussed the grouping of analysis entities into clusters with strong affinity, with each cluster representing a coarse-grained framework component. We believe that object-oriented frameworks provide a powerful underpinning for building a variety of powerful framework-based components. What differentiates an object or object-oriented framework from a component? How are object-oriented frameworks (or framework fragments) used to build components?

A.1 What Is a Component?

Let's spend some time discussing key characteristics of a component. First of all, components are not objects. While the internals of a component may be implemented using object-oriented techniques, the core properties of a component do not depend on this approach. Some of these core properties include

- Documenting clearly defined services that the component provides as well as those on which it depends

- Separating the component's external interfaces from its underlying implementation

- Providing an implementation that can be independently deployed, that is, encapsulating component data and behavior behind its external interfaces

In total, these core properties support the assertion that components are not objects. As Clemens Szyperski writes that components need not "contain classes only, or even to contain classes at all. Instead, a component could contain traditional procedures and even have global (static) variables; or it may in its entirety be realized using a functional programming approach; or using assembly language, or any other approach" [Szyperski 98].

In addition, well-defined components should perform a coherent set of functions presented in an easily digestible manner. A component that presents services supporting both currency conversion and contact management will, at a minimum, be difficult to use and manage because of its disparate functions. Even though such a component may conform to the technical definition of a component as described above, it is a less-than-optimal component because of its fragmented nature. Components should "do one thing and do it well."

You might argue that coarse components by their very nature must present a wide range of services to their potential clients. This is certainly true, and component developers clearly have to manage a balancing act between components that are so small as to be difficult to assemble with other components into a working system (that is, the coupling between components is too tight to be effective) and components that are the equivalent of a top-of-the-line Swiss Army knife—interesting to look at and contemplate but too large and cumbersome to be of any practical use.

Let's consider a warehousing component as an example of a component that fits into the middle ground between these two extremes. Our hypothetical component might present services that support primary operations for the organization deploying that component (for example, availability checks against goods held within the warehouse), those that are useful to suppliers to the organization (for example, updating lead times for various goods delivered to the warehouse), and those that allow the organization to maintain and update its warehousing capabilities within the component (for example, modifying warehouse configurations to support different goods storage approaches).

Clearly all of these services are reasonable to include within a warehousing component, but no one consumer of that component is likely to be interested in all of these services. In fact, we've already established a natural partitioning between these services in their description: operational services, supplier services, and maintenance services. In order to minimize the learning curve for consumers of our warehousing component, we should group its services into clusters of functions fronted by distinct interfaces. These interfaces present coherent and related capabilities of the component in a manner that allows consumers to effectively manage their dependencies on that component. John

Cheesman and John Daniels clearly state the benefits of grouping component functionality into distinct interfaces: "intercomponent dependencies can be restricted to individual interfaces, rather than encompass the whole component specification. This reduces the impact of change because one consumed component may replace another even if it has a different specification, as long as its specification includes the same interfaces the consuming components require" [Cheesman 00].

So, to summarize, well-defined components (for example, IBM WebSphere Business Components [IBM02]) should have the following characteristics:

- Clearly defined services that the component provides as well as those on which it depends

- Well-encapsulated implementations that can be independently deployed

- Coherent functional groupings of services into one or more interfaces presented to consumers of the component

A.2 Fine- and Coarse-Grained Components

The warehousing component described above is an example of a coarse-grained component. However, not all components are coarse-grained in nature. Java2 Enterprise Edition (J2EE), for example, introduces two types of components within its component model: SessionBeans, which align nicely to the characteristics of a coarse-grained component, and EntityBeans, which fit well with the notion of business "nouns" we've discussed in this book. These "nouns" in and of themselves can be treated as fine-grained components, either independently or within the context of a framework. Likewise, the IBM SanFrancisco frameworks' Foundation layer provides direct support for fine-grained components through its Entity concept. Typical IBM SanFrancisco–based implementations use IBM SanFrancisco's Command infrastructure, also provided by its Foundation layer, to build up coarse-grained component "shells" around these fine-grained components.

A.3 Building Coarse-Grained Components

As we've already mentioned, component implementations can vary widely. Our interest for this book is in how to use object-oriented frameworks (regardless of whether the elements of those frameworks have been implemented as fine-grained components or simple objects) to build coarse-grained components. The development cycle for coarse-grained components is no different than that of any other successful software engineering process and includes iterative cycles of requirements, analysis, design, implementation, and testing. Fine-grained framework objects or components used to implement the coarse-gained components are identified as part of the design of the coarse-grained component. These elements need to be at least partially developed before the coarse-grained components are implemented. Depending on how extensively you wish to reuse existing framework elements, you can consider tradeoffs between directly implementing coarse-grained components and building or reusing new fine-grained objects or components. To use a manufacturing analogy, when building a bicycle, you could build the frame directly from raw tubing (or even form the tubing out of sheet metal), or you could use partially or fully assembled frames that come from another internal or external supplier. This is no different than a coarse-grained component developer choosing either to develop a new collection class for internal use from scratch or to source a collection class from a preexisting class library. Because the component's interface and implementation are independent, we can make this type of tradeoff. In addition, a developer of a coarse-grained component could first provide a prototypical, custom-built implementation and then replace that implementation with one that uses (or reuses) fine-grained objects or components as they become available as long as the interface remains the same.

In the software component design process, we have developed guidelines implemented in the following four steps of the development cycle:

1. Define business requirements and use case scenarios.
2. Decompose business requirements into coarse-grained components and associated fine-grained business objects or components.
3. Map to and/or design fine-grained business objects or components.
4. Build coarse-grained business components from the underlying fine-grained implementations.

Defining Business Requirements

The key to successfully developing business components is using business rules and requirements to drive the creation of the business components. In our development model, where coarse-grained components are comprised of fine-grained components or objects, we initially use business rules and requirements to define coarse-grained components within the business domain.

Decomposing Business Requirements

Once we have established our core set of business requirements, we can begin to decompose those requirements into functional clusters—the beginnings of our coarse-grained component definitions. After decomposing business rules and requirements into coarse-grained business components, we must further decompose these coarse-grained component definitions into their underlying fine-grained business components. Once again, this decomposition should be driven by the requirements as documented by use case scenarios [Jacobson 92]. As we model fine-grained business components, the scenarios we develop become part of an analysis model. The challenge is to distribute business behavior associated with the coarse-grained components across the various fine-grained business entities defined during analysis. Often, this fine-grained modeling step occurs in tight iteration with coarse-grained component decomposition (see the Eating the Elephant pattern, Section 5.1).

Mapping to and/or Designing Fine-Grained Business Components

Because our interest is in reusing an existing framework, we now begin the process of mapping to those framework elements. If the framework we are using is well-documented, we can begin this mapping process by comparing the requirements we've just developed against the documented framework requirements. Framework traceability allows us to follow our mapped requirements to specific fine-grained framework objects or components that partially or fully meet our needs. Where the framework leaves gaps, we need to augment its capabilities with additional fine-grained objects or components and adaptation of framework elements through their defined extension points.

Building Coarse-Grained Business Components

As we've already mentioned, coarse-grained business components can be built in a number of ways. Since the interface is independent of the implementation, the component consumer does not have to change its usage when the implementation changes. This means that we can implement the coarse-grained component by using other coarse-grained components, by using fine-grained components, or by wrapping other systems. The choice of one implementation approach over another may not be clear when we first implement a coarse-grained component.

The true power of well-designed fine-grained and coarse-grained components is evident when considering the next application (or product) in a particular business domain. With a well-composed set of reusable fine-grained and coarse-grained components in hand, the analysis mapping process (as we described above) can identify many already-built business components which can then be tuned to specific needs when implementing the coarse-grained component.

Appendix

B

The IBM SanFrancisco Frameworks Development Process

In the Alles in Ordnung pattern (see Section 3.1), we emphasized the importance of selecting and deploying a well-defined development process across your framework development team. In this appendix, we include a high-level description of the development process we used for the IBM SanFrancisco business content development teams. We are not holding up this process as the perfect process that you must use. For some of you, this process may be too heavy (especially for small framework projects); for others, your corporate culture may demand a more rigorous development process. Our purpose in including this appendix is merely to show you one real-life example of a process that worked in a large, distributed development environment.

As you read this process, keep in mind that it is a framework development (production) process, not a framework usage (consumption) process. Consumers of a framework could follow a development process similar to that described here, but with three significant differences (see Chapter 9).

1. Framework consumers are likely to produce fewer supporting documentation artifacts than framework producers.

2. Framework consumers need to introduce explicit mapping against framework documentation artifacts wherever they exist throughout the development process. The earlier mapping is introduced into the development process, the greater the likelihood that the framework will be used to its fullest capabilities.

3. Framework consumers need to base their documentation on associated framework documentation. For example, when mapping against framework

requirements documents, those documents should be used as a starting point for application documentation that expands on those requirements.

B.1 Process Flow

The overall flow through the process is described below. The process may proceed sequentially or iteratively through each stage. Some stages may be combined or performed in parallel. Developers may use an iterative process whereby certain elements of a functional unit (also known as a feature), having already progressed to a more advanced stage, reenter a previous stage for revision. In this situation, you must adhere to the requirements for the stage being reentered and all subsequent stages. However, if the revision is localized, required activities (such as reviews) may be limited to the revised portion. Developers may also design a portion of a function needed for a functional unit and then iterate through the activities, adding more functions until the functional unit is complete. It is the responsibility of the developers along with their team leader to determine when combining or iteration is appropriate and to what extent the activities of a stage must be performed during each iteration. A component test and a component regression test are performed on a complete functional unit.

Overview of Process Activities

- Requirements development
- Scenario development
- Scenario handoff meeting
- Design
- Combined review
- Code and feature test
- Code review
- Integration
- Build verification test
- Component test
- Component regression test

These are covered in detail below in the Process Step Details section.

Process Flow Variations

Changes to Existing Features

There sometimes is a need to change the scenario, design, code, or test cases for existing features. There are many reasons for these changes, which can range, for example, from fixing a bug to redesigning a feature to improve performance to adding Euro currency changes into everything from the scenarios on down. The entire development process described by the steps above is not needed for these changes, but no one other process can fit all these situations.

A group that includes at least the team leader, the object-oriented (OO) lead, and the assigned developer (but could include the domain lead, other developers, and the scenario author, depending on the size of the change) should determine which of the steps within the process outlined above need to be followed.

Code Fix Process

In addition to the normal development process shown above, a mechanism exists to integrate changes and fixes into already-integrated code. In general, the steps normally required by the development process prior to integration are not required for code fix integration. However, a change requiring major modification to the internals of the functional unit or, especially, to its external interface must follow the applicable portions of the normal process. The owner of the functional unit along with the team leader are responsible for deciding what constitutes a major modification and what process steps apply. The developer responsible for the code fix is required to review the change and run any test cases that identified the problem prior to integration. If no test case existed to identify the problem, one must be written (if possible within reasonable time and resource constraints) and added to the test plan for the appropriate functional unit. The originator must state the severity of the code defect. The severity level identifies how quickly a response or solution to the problem is needed. The originator may also review the code change or fix.

B.2 Process Artifacts

Process-Related Artifacts

There are a number of artifacts associated with the process.

- **Requirements**—a high-level description of what the framework is intended to do.

- **Use cases**—high-level descriptions of interactions with the framework. Although for other types of software development these start from the application user, for a framework, since there isn't a specific application, they often start from the first use of what is provided by the framework.
- **Scenarios**—more detailed use cases that describe how the analysis objects work together to fulfill the requirements.
- **Analysis models**—high-level, domain-recognizable models of the objects and responsibilities of the framework solution.
- **Design models**—detailed models of the objects and responsibilities of the classes that are used to implement the analysis diagrams.
- **Interaction diagrams**—diagrams that show the interactions of the design-level objects. This is usually in support of a particular method call.
- **Feature test cases**—test cases that test a feature in isolation. Often these test cases, especially those that can be automated, are used as part of the build verification test.
- **Component test cases**—test cases that test the entire framework product. These are often used for the component regression test to ensure that the framework is still working correctly after a change.

User Documentation Artifacts

It is important during the development of the design and code deliverables not to overlook providing the technical input into the user documentation. The IBM SanFrancisco frameworks deliver the following types of user documentation that relate to the business content.

- **Extension guide**—a how-to guide for extending the framework.
- **Functional overview**—a description of the overall function provided by the framework.
- **Glossary**—a list of terms with definitions.
- **User guides**—domain-centric descriptions of the functions provided by the framework. These approach the framework from a domain perspective and are where we expect domain experts to gain an understanding of the framework so they can determine how they can use it to build their applications.
- **Persistent object planning guide**—a document that provides information about persisting the frameworks classes and their extensions.

The user guides require the most input from the development team, but the other documentation shouldn't be overlooked.

In this process, developers provide the raw material for user documentation. This raw material is called *user document artifacts*. The development process results in units that are handed over to the information development team, which edits, spell checks, links together, and bundles the units into the product documentation provided to users of the IBM SanFrancisco frameworks.

B.3 Process Participants

- **Domain expert**—a team member with expertise in the domain area of interest. Among other responsibilities, domain experts write requirements and detailed scenarios.

- **Developer**—a software engineer responsible for design and implementation of the framework.

- **OO lead**—an expert software engineer responsible for suggesting and reviewing designs and mentoring less experienced developers.

- **Domain lead**—a domain expert with deep experience in one or more areas of the domain, responsible for reviewing requirements and detailed scenarios and mentoring less experienced domain experts.

- **Information architect**—a technical writer responsible for laying out framework documentation.

- **Information development team leader**—an experienced technical writer.

- **Development group lead**—a developer with responsibility for leadership of a small group of developers.

- **Component test team member**—a tester responsible for executing typical framework usage test cases to validate framework function.

- **Performance team member**—a developer with expertise in optimizing software performance.

- **Cross-domain architect**—a domain expert with broad experience in the domain who establishes the domain architecture of the framework, including initial partitioning of the framework into component categories. Usually this person also acts as the consistency czar (see Section 8.3).

Note: A given person may play more than one role in the process.

B.4 Process Step Details

Requirements Development

The purpose of requirements gathering is to gain an initial understanding of the domain that will be supported and how software developers will need to customize applications in that domain for different customers in different locations. This is accomplished by interviewing domain experts to learn how they do their business.

The discussions are documented in the form of use cases. Each use case illustrates a single set of interactions that produce a business result. A use case shows the flow of the business processes and operations. At times it may also identify transaction boundaries.

The requirements process should also identify where and how the use cases will vary from installation to installation. These may include points where software developers want to provide their own business logic or where country-specific differences need to be incorporated into the use case.

Once the use cases for the domain are drafted they should be reviewed with the domain experts to verify accuracy. The result of the requirements gathering is a set of use cases that describe the functions that need to be performed by the domain framework and the extension points where developers must be able to override the framework code.

Scenario Development

This stage of the process covers the definition of the scenarios that describe a particular feature. Domain experts develop the scenarios.

Scenario Development Objectives
- Create scenarios for a specified feature.

Scenario Development Participants
- Scenario writer
- Other domain experts as required
- Developers assigned to the feature
- OO lead (optional)
- Other developers as required

Scenario Development Entrance Criteria

- The domain expert is assigned to author the scenarios for a feature.
- Requirements for this feature are complete.

Scenario Development Activities

- An author (usually a domain expert) is assigned to write a scenario.
- A domain peer review maybe be held, which is a "desk review" of the scenarios by other domain experts. Comments from the review are returned directly to the scenario author.
- The scenario author makes the scenarios available to the developers responsible for the feature.
- The scenario author refines the scenarios with input from the developers.

Scenario Development Exit Criteria

- The scenario author and the developers agree that the scenario is ready to be handed off. This means that it will meet the entrance criteria for a scenario handoff meeting.

Scenario Handoff Meeting

The goal of this phase is to identify the activities associated with a particular feature and ensure that the developers (or design team members) who will create the design understand the scenario. The handoff should not be considered complete until the developers think they understand the scenario enough to do the design.

This phase is also used to establish what new user document artifacts or changes to existing user document artifacts are required in the library of information. User guide changes are typical, but changes might also be necessary in, for example, the extensions guide, the functional overview, the glossary, or the persistent object planning guide.

This phase may be skipped if the developers and team leader agree that a meeting is not required.

Scenario Handoff Objectives

- Discuss the high-level design and design patterns that should be considered.
- Gain sufficient understanding of scenarios to begin the design process.

- Begin to identify detailed dependencies on other features.
- If the schedule for a feature is broken into partial and full development, identify the portion of the feature that makes up the partial development effort. If a scenario is broken into partial development (for example, stubbed methods will be temporarily provided for portions of the feature), the developers and team leader will decide how much of the full process should be applied to the partial scenario.
- Identify any errors in the scenarios before design starts.
- Reach agreement between the development team and the information development team on changes that need to be made to existing information and what new information is needed, if any.

Scenario Handoff Participants

- Scenario writer or domain expert (if the scenario writer is not available)
- OO lead
- Domain lead
- Designers/developers assigned to implement the scenarios
- Information architect
- Information development team leader
- Development group lead (optional)
- Component test team member (optional)
- Other developers as required

Scenario Handoff Materials

The following information should be available:

- The scenario document
- The requirements document
- The analysis level design (class diagrams)
- Any existing design-level class diagrams or information
- Dependency information (what this scenario depends on, including the dependencies that the developer knows) in a format determined by the developer
- A list of the user document artifacts required to be created or changed

Scenario Handoff Entrance Criteria

- All required participants should have read the scenario prior to the meeting. When scheduling the meeting allow time for preparation or get permission from the participants to expedite the review.

Scenario Handoff Possible Outcomes

- **No changes to scenarios required**—scenario development is complete. Design begins.
- **Minor changes to scenarios required**—the design phase can proceed if the developer, OO lead, and domain expert agree that the required scenario changes are not major or that they can be isolated from most of the design. The domain expert or scenario writer must correct the scenario in a reasonable time frame.
- **Reinspection required**—another complete scenario handoff meeting will be required.

Scenario Handoff Exit Criteria

- The developer understands the scenario well enough to proceed with the design.
- Any scenario changes identified during the handoff meeting are corrected or will be soon after the scenario handoff.
- Participants should agree on the high-level design.
- Once completed, all changes to scenarios must be approved by the component owner or delegate.
- The developer and/or domain expert understands what user document artifacts need to be created or updated as a result of this feature.

Design

Design Objectives

- Complete the feature design.
- Manage design/code dependencies in other features. The goal is to identify dependencies early so that they can be managed.
- Complete the feature test plan.
- Apply well-understood design patterns.
- Create the new and updated user document artifacts for the feature.

Design Participants

- Developer (may be a design team)
- OO lead (as needed)
- Domain lead (as needed)
- Test team (as needed)
- Other peer developers as required

Design Entrance Criteria

- The scenario handoff is complete.

Design Exit Criteria

- The design model for the feature is fully documented.
- All necessary design diagrams are produced.
- If the design is complex, consider providing multiple design diagrams that offer different views of the design.
- All classes are fully documented.
- All methods are fully documented.
- Collaboration diagrams are provided for complex scenarios as necessary.
- The design has been peer reviewed by another developer who is not part of your design team. Where possible, find a peer reviewer who either has designed a similar feature or who has to design a similar feature in the future.
- The feature test plan is complete, and the test matrix is laid out with test scenarios and variations documented.
- The test plan has been peer reviewed by a domain expert.
- User document artifacts have been written and peer reviewed.

Combined Review

The purpose of this meeting is to review the output of the design step. Ensure ample time is given to reviewers to review the material. Expedited reviews should first be agreed to by all reviewers.

This phase may be skipped if the developer and team leader agree that it is not required.

Combined Review Objectives

- Verify that the design and scenarios are correct and that they logically match.
- Verify that the feature test plan is sufficient.
- Look for performance impacts.
- Verify the use of design patterns and identify new or potential patterns.
- Identify the component test team member responsible for the feature.

Combined Review Participants

- Scenario writer or domain expert
- Developer/design team
- OO lead
- Domain lead
- Group lead (if applicable)
- Component test team member
- Performance team member (at least notified of progress through written communication)
- Cross-domain architect (at least notified of progress through written communication)
- Moderator

Combined Review Entrance Criteria

- The design is complete (exit criteria for the design phase have been met).
- User document artifacts are ready or an agreement has been made to review them separately.
- All required reviewers have reviewed the review materials.

Combined Review Materials

The following documents should be distributed to local participants.

- The scenario document
- The requirements document
- The analysis-level design (class diagrams)
- All design-level class diagrams
- Design class specifications (including methods)

- Collaboration diagrams
- The feature test plan
- User document artifacts (unless their review has been separated from the combined review)
- Dependency information (what this scenario depends on, including the dependencies that the developer knows)

Combined Review Possible Outcomes

- **No changes to design required**—design is complete. Coding and feature testing can proceed.
- **Minor changes to design required**—changes must be made to the design model and/or test sources. Design is complete when the developer and OO lead agree that changes are complete. Coding and feature testing can proceed in parallel with the changes to the design model and test sources.
- **Reinspection required**—another complete combined review is required.

Combined Review Exit Criteria

- Any changes identified in the design documentation during review are corrected or the team leader and developer have determined when the changes will be corrected.
- User document artifacts changes due to design changes are identified.

Code and Feature Test

The goal of this phase is to produce the actual Java code for the feature and the feature tests.

Code and Feature Test Objectives

- Generated code is generated.
- Nongenerated code is implemented.
- The feature test plan is implemented.
- Major paths are tested. Note that feature testing is not as complete as traditional unit testing. In other words, not all areas of the code require testing. There are two reasons for this: (1) much of the code is automatically generated and does not require complete testing and (2) since this is a framework that will be extended by the customer, not all of the code paths are complete.

Code and Feature Test Participants
- Developer/design team
- Domain expert (as needed)
- OO lead (as needed)
- Other developers (as needed)

Code and Feature Test Entrance Criteria
- The combined review is completed.

Code and Feature Checklist for Integrating Code
- The code compiles correctly.
- The code conforms to the design. (This may require modification of code-generator directives in the design to get good results.)
- The code does not break dependencies from other features.
- When providing early support for dependencies, stubbed methods return "reasonable" results. Stubbed method behavior should be negotiated with the user of the method.
- The code has been tested using the feature test plan.

Code and Feature Test Exit Criteria
- The design has been fully implemented.
- The feature test plan for the feature has been fully implemented.
- All test cases for the feature test pass.
- All test cases can be run without user intervention.
- The code and test cases have been integrated.
- Selected test cases have been identified for the build verification test and added to its run list.
- The Javadoc is complete.

Code Review

All code should be considered for review. Code reviews are held only for selected sections of the code. Code to be reviewed is identified by the developer and the OO lead or delegate. The developer is responsible for setting up the code review meeting or desk review. Candidates for code that may be reviewed include

- Complex hand-generated code
- Performance-sensitive code

The Javadoc for the feature should also be included in the code review.

For all review comments that are not incorporated into the code, the author of the comment should be told why the comment wasn't accepted and the OO lead should approve.

If the code review is a desk review in which everyone puts their comments into or on one copy of the code, the OO lead should be the last person to review the code. This lets him or her address comments not only to the code but also to the comments of the other reviewers.

Code Review Participants

- Developer
- OO lead
- Performance team members (as needed)
- Other developers (as needed)

Code Review Entrance Criteria

Code to be reviewed is complete and has been identified for review by the developer responsible for the code.

Code Review Exit Criteria

- All participant comments have been received and responded to.

Integration

Integration is the stage used to bring a feature together with other features and with the previously integrated IBM SanFrancisco code base. Once code has entered integration, it is available for builds with all the IBM SanFrancisco code that has reached integration and for the build verification test. Once integrated, the code is under fix control.

Integration Entrance Criteria

- All exit criteria for the combined review and feature test stages must be complete (exceptions are allowed).

Integration Activities
- Integrate all code available for the feature into the current build.

Integration Exit Criteria
- Code features have been integrated.

Build Verification Test

The purpose of the build verification test is to verify that all integrated code is working properly together. Feature test cases are used in order to provide this level of testing. Typically these are the feature tests that can be automatically run and verified.

Build Verification Test Entrance Criteria
- All exit criteria for the combined review and feature test stages must be complete (exceptions are allowed).
- All feature test code test cases and associated drivers have been integrated.

Build Verification Test Activities
- Add the new test case to the run list for the framework component after ensuring that the test case will run in the build verification test environment.

Build Verification Test Exit Criteria
- The new test bucket for the build verification test runs successfully in the integrated driver.

Component Test

The component test is the first level of testing done by an external party (that is, not the developer of the feature). It tests the public interfaces of the component. No scaffold test code (code that exists only to allow the test case to run) can be used during this stage.

Component Test Objectives
- Test the feature in an environment where it is integrated with other features. This level of test should use the component-tested level of the prerequisite features and should not use scaffold code. It should assure that the interactions between features work as specified.

- Test data level integration between features. Where an object is created by one feature and used by another feature it should be created using the component-tested level of the prerequisite feature.

- Test the feature from a usage viewpoint. This involves analyzing how a user would interact with an integrated set of features and planning/ executing test cases to verify that the user actions produce the expected results.

- Validate that the feature can run on a single platform or in a client/ server environment. The cases created for the component test should not presume a specific configuration. The intent is for them to be reusable in a multi-client/server environment for product testing.

- Validate persistence.

Component Test Entrance Criteria

For test plan and test case definition:

- Development documentation is complete to the level required for the combined review to be held.

- The component tester has studied the requirements, design model, and scenarios for the feature.

For test execution:

- The feature test is complete and the code is integrated.

- The build verification test for this feature was successful.

- The test plan and test cases have been reviewed.

- The test cases have been implemented and compiled.

Component Test Activities

- Create and review a test plan that lists the cases and iterations to be tested for the feature.

- Review the test plan with the component test team lead, a domain person, and the feature developer or development team leader. No strict format for the review is imposed. However, the review must be sufficient to ensure that the objectives of this stage are met.

- Review the test case code.

- Execute the test plan.

Component Test Exit Criteria

For test plan and test case definition:

- A test plan has been created and reviewed.
- Test cases are reviewed.

For test execution:

- All test cases for the feature pass without user intervention.
- All issues raised during the test plan review are resolved.
- Any failures with fixes deferred to another release (or fix pack) have a tracking record written and assigned.
- The test plan documentation is updated to reflect the results of the resolved issues.

Component Regression Test

This stage of the process covers the final verification of code correctness after completion of all other stages of the process. The purpose of this stage is to verify that no defects were introduced during the process to previously working code and that the component tests run successfully on all supported platforms and databases.

Component Regression Test Entrance Criteria

- All exit criteria for the component test and code review stages are met.

OR

- A large percentage of the component test cases (as determined or approved by the manager or team leader responsible for the functional unit) have been successfully completed. That the component tester claims attempts and successes is sufficient evidence the manager or team leader has approved the start of the component regression test.

Component Regression Test Activities

- All test cases for the component test run during the component test stage are rerun on all supported platforms and databases unless the testing before the component regression test indicates that only a subset is required.

Component Regression Test Exit Criteria

- All tests must run successfully unless the fix is deferred.
- All nondeferred tracking records created for found defects must be closed or be marked as complete for the current fix release.
- Any failures with fixes deferred to another release must have a tracking record written and assigned.

Bibliography

[Ambler 99]   Scott W. Ambler. *Process Patterns: Building Large-Scale Systems Using Object Technology.* Cambridge, UK: Cambridge University Press, 1999.

[Beck 00]   Kent Beck. *Extreme Programming Explained: Embrace Change.* Reading, MA: Addison-Wesley, 2000.

[Beck 02]   Kent Beck and Erich Gamma. *JUnit (Java Unit Test Case Framework).* Accessed online at http://members.pingnet.ch/gamma/junit.htm.

[Booch 94]   Grady Booch. *Object-Oriented Analysis and Design with Applications.* Redwood City, CA: Benjamin/Cummings, 1994.

[Carey 00]   James Carey, Brent Carlson, and Tim Graser. *SanFrancisco Design Patterns: Blueprints for Business Software.* Reading, MA: Addison-Wesley, 2000.

[Carnegie Mellon 02] Carnegie Mellon Software Engineering Institute's Capability Maturity Model for Software Web site at http://www.sei.cmu.edu/cmm.

[Cheesman 01]   John Cheesman and John Daniels. *UML Components: A Simple Process for Specifying Component-Based Software.* Reading, MA: Addison-Wesley, 2001.

[Cline 95]   Marshall P. Cline and Greg A. Lomow. *C++ FAQs.* Reading, MA: Addison-Wesley, 1995.

[Cockburn 98]   Alistair Cockburn. *Surviving Object-Oriented Projects: A Manager's Guide.* Reading, MA: Addison-Wesley, 1998.

[Cockburn 00]   Alistair Cockburn. *Writing Effective Use Cases.* Reading, MA: Addison-Wesley, 2000.

[Dennison 90]   Bill Dennison and Roger Kirk. *Do, Review, Learn, Apply: A Simple Guide to Experiential Learning.* Oxford, UK: Blackwell Education, 1990.

[Fowler 97]   Martin Fowler. *Analysis Patterns: Reusable Object Models.* Reading, MA: Addison-Wesley, 1997.

[Fowler 99]   Martin Fowler and Kent Beck. *Refactoring: Improving the Design of Existing Code.* Reading, MA: Addison-Wesley, 1999.

[Fowler 00]   Martin Fowler and Kendall Scott. *UML Distilled.* Reading, MA: Addison-Wesley, 2000.

[Gamma 94]   Erich Gamma, Richard Helm, Ralph Johnson, and John Vlissides. *Design Patterns: Elements of Reusable Object-Oriented Software.* Reading, MA: Addison-Wesley, 1994.

[IBM 99]   IBM Corporation. *IBM SanFrancisco Warehouse Management User Guide.* IBM SanFrancisco Release 1.3 Evaluation CD. Armonk, NY: IBM, 1999.

[IBM 02]   IBM Corporation. WebSphere Business Components Web site at http://www.ibm.com/software/webservers/components.

[Jacobson 92]   Ivar Jacobson, Magnus Christerson, Patrik Jonsson, and Gunnar Overgaard. *Object-Oriented Software Engineering: A Use Case Driven Approach.* Reading, MA: Addison-Wesley, 1992.

[Jacobson 99]   Ivar Jacobson, Grady Booch, and James Rumbaugh. *The Unified Software Development Process.* Reading, MA: Addison-Wesley, 1999.

[Jaufmann 00]   Edwin Jaufmann, Jr., and Daniel Logan. The use of IBM SanFrancisco's core business processes in human resource scheduling. *IBM Systems Journal*, 39(2):285–292, 2000.

[Johnson 02]   Ralph Johnson's Frameworks Home Page at http://st-www.cs.uiuc.edu/users/johnson/frameworks.html.

[LogicLibrary 02]   LogicLibrary Web site at http://www.logiclibrary.com.

[Meyers 97]   Scott Meyers. *Effective C++: 50 Ways to Improve Your Programs and Design*. Reading, MA: Addison-Wesley, 1997.

[Miller 56]   G. A. Miller. The magical number seven plus or minus two: Some limits on our capacity for processing information. *Psychological Review*, 63:81–97, 1956.

[Monday 99]   Paul Monday, James Carey, and Mary Dangler. *SanFrancisco Component Framework: An Introduction*. Reading, MA: Addison-Wesley, 1999.

[O'Connor 93]   Joseph O'Connor and John Seymour. *Introducing NLP*. Wellingborough, Northants, UK: The Aquarian Press, 1993.

[Pree 95]   Wolfgang Pree. *Design Patterns for Object-Oriented Software Development*. Reading, MA: Addison-Wesley, 1995.

[Pree 01]   Wolfgang Pree and Kai Koskimies. *Framelets: Small and Loosely Coupled Frameworks*. Accessed online at http://www.softwareresearch.net/publications/J011.pdf.

[Rising 00]   Linda Rising. *The Patterns Almanac 2000*. Reading, MA: Addison-Wesley, 2000.

[Scholtes 96]   Peter R. Scholtes, Brian L. Joiner, and Barbara J. Streibel. *The Team Handbook*, 2nd Edition. Madison, WI: Oriel, 1996.

[Szyperski 98]   Clemens Szyperski. *Component Software: Beyond Object-Oriented Programming*. Reading, MA: Addison-Wesley, 1998.

Index

Also Available from Addison-Wesley

SanFrancisco™ Design Patterns
Blueprints for Business Software

By James Carey, Brent Carlson, and Tim Graser

"This book is priceless because it explains why the developers of SanFrancisco™ designed things the way they did. As such, it takes a good hard look at the problems involved in writing flexible business software and the patterns inherent in the solutions this team came up with."

—Martin Fowler

Design patterns are the heart of SanFrancisco. Whether building a business application in SanFrancisco or from scratch, the patterns identified in this book will help you build flexibility, power, and strength into your business applications. This book follows the format established by the seminal *Design Patterns*, with a case study providing a business context for patterns running throughout the book. The authors focus on the generic use of these patterns using SanFrancisco as an example. With this book as your guide, you will learn how to use and extend these patterns within the context of a business application's requirements.

0-201-61644-0 • Paperback • 400 pages • ©2000

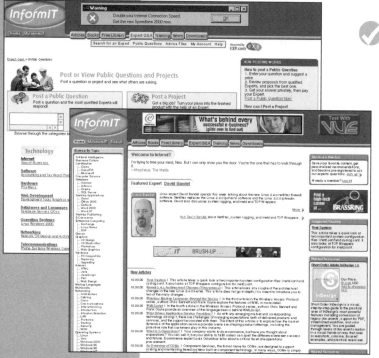

Register Your Book

at www.aw.com/cseng/register

You may be eligible to receive:

- Advance notice of forthcoming editions of the book
- Related book recommendations
- Chapter excerpts and supplements of forthcoming titles
- Information about special contests and promotions throughout the year
- Notices and reminders about author appearances, tradeshows, and online chats with special guests

Contact us

If you are interested in writing a book or reviewing manuscripts prior to publication, please write to us at:

Editorial Department
Addison-Wesley Professional
75 Arlington Street, Suite 300
Boston, MA 02116 USA
Email: AWPro@aw.com

Visit us on the Web: http://www.aw.com/cseng